Letters to a Grandson

Letters
to a Grandson

LORD HOME

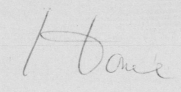

September 1983.

COLLINS
8 Grafton Street, London W1
1983

William Collins Sons & Co Ltd
London · Glasgow · Sydney · Auckland
Toronto · Johannesburg

British Library Cataloguing in Publication Data

Home, Alec Douglas-Home *Baron*
Letters to a grandson.
1. Home, Alec Douglas-Home *Baron*
2. Prime ministers—Great Britain—Biography
I. Title
941.085′6′0924   DA591.H6

ISBN 0-00-217061-2

First Published 1983
© Lord Home 1983

Set in Bembo
Made and Printed in Great Britain by
William Collins Sons & Co Ltd Glasgow

My dear Matthew,

I hope you don't object to my making our correspondence – or rather my side of it – public. I promise not to publish anything of yours without first obtaining permission.

INTRODUCTION

When you were staying with us for the Christmas holidays and we were looking through the eighty-eight volumes of your Grandmother's scrap-books, two thoughts struck me. The first that I had been alive for a very long time, during which a lot had happened; and the second that I was about your age and away at school when I began to take notice of national and international affairs.

Today you would hardly recognize the Britain of those times. We had enjoyed the hundred years of unbroken peace which was flatteringly called the 'Pax Britannica'; we had an Empire on which 'the sun never set'; and we had the power because our navy really did rule the waves; and we never had any trouble with the Pound Sterling which was as 'safe as the Bank of England'.

When I went to school in 1913 everything looked to be plain-sailing, and then without warning we were plunged into war with Germany.

I remember how lightly we took it. August 4th, 1914, was like a Bank Holiday, with a rush to the Colours, and confident predictions that the war would be finished by Christmas. Patriotism was indignant. How did the Kaiser – a grandson of Queen Victoria – dare to challenge her Imperial power? His son, 'little Willie', with his long nose and bullet-head, with his military cap with its arrogant brim, was the toast of all the caricaturists, and so we laughed on our way, certain of victory. It was to be five slogging years before it came, and seven hundred thousand were to be killed from Britain alone. So in the twinkling of an eye the fortunes of men and nations changed.

The story of it all would have been too long to tell before you went away, but I thought that if I wrote you a letter from time to time, the exercise would sharpen my memory and might be of interest to you.

As we go along you will see the difficulty of trying to identify the lessons to be drawn from the 20th century wars and the short interval between them, for almost all of them underline the fact that man has learnt virtually nothing at all in two thousand years!

The advice 'Put not your trust in Princes' seems to be as valid now as it was then, nor does it seem to matter whether the 'Prince' is a Czar or a Kaiser, a self-styled Dictator like Hitler, a Stalin claiming to be acting in the name of the 'common man' or an Ayatollah dealing out violence in the guise of religion. The urge for power and the compulsion to use it at the expense of his neighbour is apparently rooted deep in human nature.

Perhaps that is not surprising if man stems from the animal kingdom, but it means that the peace–keeper is working in a hostile environment where moral considerations go by the board.

The instinct of the Christian, for example, leans towards tolerance and trust, and turning the other cheek to the man next door. That posture is contained in the ethic that human society is destined to evolve towards the better life in which man is the beneficiary.

So far, however, on the hard evidence, the peace-maker may have to rethink his philosophy, for the two wars have shown that good is not automatically blessed, and that security is not guaranteed by good intentions. Quite the contrary, for conciliation, negotiation, compromise, tolerance – all the civilized words in the Christian and democratic vocabulary – have too often turned out to be a trap. It is doubtless to the credit of man that he has sought a better way to keep the peace than that of alliances, and the balance of power by promoting organizations dedicated to supplying security through an International Police Force; but trust in the League of Nations turned out to be misplaced, and the United Nations so far has no relevance in the setting of the rivalry of great powers. Neither Covenants nor Charters have been able to guarantee peace.

Does all that sound to you like the lament of a period pessimist who has got out of bed the wrong side? Well, I will plead guilty to such a mood if and when as the tale unfolds we find promise and hope of better things to come.

Anyhow here goes.

PS Don't answer until I have finished my story. I remember at school that letter-writing was one of the worst of the chores. There was always something better to do.

Letter One

It is difficult to know where to start the story, but
I am going to do so with my father. First, because
he was a soldier in the 1914 war, and secondly,
because he had friends in politics from whom I
used to pick up scraps of knowledge when they
came to stay at The Hirsel.

To mark the change between then and now I
must tell you that he went to war on his horse!
I remember long arguments before the cavalry
were converted into infantry, or artillery, or
armoured vehicles.

The advantage of the horse in previous wars
had been mobility, but no one had yet thought
of replacing the horse with the tank. They did
so in 1916, but so tentative was the experiment
that there were too few spare parts to rescue the
casualties from wear and tear, and the technical
and tactical advantage was lost.

So the German, French and British infantry
dug themselves into the earth and my memory of
the war is of the armies engaged in trench war-

fare, and literally stuck in the mud. This was true of the allies and of the Germans, for none of the Generals had any strategy or tactics other than a static war of attrition. Time and again over the four years hundreds would pour out of the trenches and 'over the top' as it was called, and be caught in the coils of barbed wire and be massacred in a hail of bullets and shrapnel.

It will seem inconceivable to you, but at the battle of Loos alone – and it lasted a week – the casualties were 45,000 men, and the gain 100 yards.

The soldiers marched into battle singing 'Pack up your troubles in your old kit bag, and smile, smile, smile', or 'It's a long way to Tipperary', and at school we used to buttress our morale by the caricatures in *Punch*, and by repeating the music-hall quips of the day.

But alongside the defensive shell of gaiety I remember the young poet, Siegfried Sassoon, writing:

'I'd like to see a tank come down the stalls
   Lurching to rag-time tunes and 'Home
      Sweet Home',
And there'd be no more jokes in music-
   halls
   To mock the riddled corpses round
      Bapaume'.

If your contemporaries at school are like my generation you will agree that boys are neither introspective nor morbid, but during those years of war there was never a day when we did not go to bed with anxiety, and wake up with apprehension, for week by week a father or a brother or a family friend would die.

And when the Bank Holiday mood with which the war had begun waned, and the forecasts of a walk-over were falsified whom did we blame?

Our Christian God for creating a world which was capable of such cruelty and hate? That thought intruded, but we tucked it away, for the Church had taught us that the gift of free-will had been bestowed upon man. Given the option of peace man had chosen war. That was baffling and demoralizing, but we took comfort in the thought that we were fighting against those who had broken the Christian code of conduct towards his neighbour.

We therefore harnessed God to our side, for did not Britain stand for justice and right?

Did we blame the politicians whose business it was to anticipate danger, and to provide national security? There at least we could derive some comfort and reassurance, for everyone knew of the efforts of Sir Edward Grey, the

Foreign Secretary, to avert war and to save the peace.

I recall that in the post-mortems which he conducted with my father that he had but two doubts. The first as to whether his warnings to the Germans had been early enough, and explicit enough to convince them that Britain would fight, and the second whether he could have been more successful in contriving what he used to refer to as the 'equilibrium of Europe'. By that he meant the possibility of including Russia in an alliance which would, with Britain and France, bring about a better balance of power which would cause Germany to think.

With the benefit of hindsight it appears that his experience with the Czar's government was not very different from those of our negotiations with the Communists before Hitler's war. Ambivalence and prevarication and suspicion and deception were the techniques which the Russians employed.

Russia was and is a big fish in terms of power, but she is not easily netted into an alliance with democracy.

Those who attracted the greatest criticism were the Generals. A lot of it was unfair, for right up until the outbreak of war Britain's military strategy was geared to the defence of the widespread Empire, so that the navy had the precedence and the army was the Cinderella of the Services.

Lord Haig, the Commander of the allied armies in the last two years of the war, who was another of my father's friends, used to express his apprehension as to our ability to fulfil these ubiquitous obligations while simultaneously raising an expeditionary force to fight on the continent of Europe. His fear was reinforced by his opinion that the French were unlikely to be reliable allies. Haig, when he succeeded to the High Command, employed the same military tactics of mass attack and attrition as his predecessors. Had he seen a better way he would certainly have adopted it for I remember him as one of the most humane of men.

Those war years were a searing experience for old and young, and they were a sombre curtain on an age of continuing prosperity and peace.

Of course in crisis and in war the dilemma of laughter or tears is never far away. Years afterwards, when I went to New York with Mr Harold Macmillan, and we were deep in serious discussions with the Americans and Russians on the limitation of nuclear weapons, the following story was circulating in the corridors of the United Nations.

It concerned the offer by the Devil of one wish each to President Kennedy, Chairman Kruschev and Mr Macmillan.

'Your wish, Mr President?'
    '100 megaton bombs.'
'And yours, Chairman Kruschev?'
    '200 megaton bombs.'
'And yours, Mr Macmillan?'
    'A whisky and soda, please, but serve the
    other two gentlemen first.'

So it goes on. Does man ever learn?

Out of victory in 1918 there arose a question which was greatly to affect the attitude of the British to the Germans over the years which were to separate 1918 and 1931.

Mr Lloyd George, the dynamic Welshman who was the political architect of victory, proposed to squeeze the Germans 'until the pips squeaked'. The majority of the people of Britain, however, having done the job and won the fight, were ready, perhaps too ready, to forgive and forget. The task of the peace-makers was formidable and delicate indeed. If the Germans were 'squeezed' too far they would be an economic liability to Europe, and were all too likely to harbour resentment and thoughts of revenge, while if they were let off too lightly they would not recognize the enormity of the crime of which they had been guilty, and their arrogance could easily have sprung up again.

Lord Robert Cecil, who was Britain's representative at the Peace Conference at Versailles, used to talk with my father of those horns of the statesman's dilemma.

You would greatly have enjoyed him. Physically and intellectually he was the original egghead with a huge domed cranium, obviously bursting with brains, and with a big hooked nose like a magnified Mr Punch! He was very tall and he had a habit of sliding down on his diningroom chair until his chin was almost resting on the table.

It was from him that I first learned of the idea of an international body to act as police to secure peace and order among the nations. With the help and backing of President Wilson of the United States, this concept was to take shape as the League of Nations. Everyone was full of excitement and enthusiasm, for was not this recognition that the time to end all wars had arrived, and with it the millennium?

I remember that Lord Rosebery, who had been Prime Minister, was one of the few who felt that in a world upon which so much hate and propaganda had been let loose, democracy and the

essential freedoms would have a struggle to survive, but he was one of a very few pessimists,
and the rest jumped on to the platform of collective security.

Churchill, Baldwin and Chamberlain were
full of enthusiasm – the same men who, because
the dream collapsed, were to play the lead in the
next international drama to be staged.

Their names will indicate to you that our hopes
of peace and quiet were to be dashed a second
time; but that was not yet, and most people
thought that Utopia was round the corner. That
was a mistake, for winds of change which were
blowing were full of portent.

Wealth measured in billions had been blown
into the air; the Colonies which composed the
British Empire had caught the fever of independence; a Socialist party in Britain had been
born and was becoming a political force; while
Russia had been taken over by militant Communists who had the fervour of religious cru-
saders.

Nothing in fact, economically, politically or
socially, would ever be the same again.

Letter Two

On re-reading my last letter I felt a bit guilty at inflicting on you so much woe, but that is what the world of my youth was like. I wish I could say that man has learned the plain lesson that war is a futile way of settling disputes, but one glance round the world will convince you that he has not.

I hope, however, I can make one claim for Britain as a Christian and democratic society. We did not provoke the Kaiser, and we bent over backwards to conciliate Hitler to the point when I and others were labelled 'guilty men'. Nor, I think you will agree if I skip the years, can the democracies be accused of harbouring aggressive intentions against Communist Russia – the most likely aggressors of today.

My attitude to them has always been that if the Russians want Communism, let them have it, and enjoy it, or stew in its juice as the case may be. I only object when they try and shove their doctrine down other people's throats by force.

But before I go into all that, why did Britain fight in 1914, and again in 1939, even though all our instincts revolted against trial by war, and we longed to settle for peace? It was quite simply that both those German leaders, Kaiser Wilhelm and Hitler (who, incidentally, were as different as chalk from cheese) insisted on trying to dominate the centre of the Continent of Europe by force.

Philip of Spain and Napoleon had tried to do the same thing, and the British people had felt bound to oppose them rather than lose their chosen way of life, and so it was with those two.

Rather luckily we had once experienced in our own domestic history the penalties which follow when power is concentrated in the hands of an autocrat.

You will remember from your history books how the reaction of the educated and politically conscious curbed the claim to divine right by the Stuart Kings, and that (apart from our Scottish invasion of England!) Britain only had one Civil War. But that equipped the British people with a keen nose for sniffing out tyranny, and proved to them that the greatest threat to the freedoms of ordinary men and women are those over-bearing few who refuse to recognize restraint in the use of power.

They now know that, whether as in the old days it was King or Church or Barons or Cartels, or as today a Trade Union which seeks to set itself above the law, that if freedom is to be preserved the people must speak and act in time. That is a gut reaction. In 1914 it was dormant after 100 years of peace, but instinctively it rose to the top.

The Kaiser was a spoilt and arrogant bully, who wanted everyone to get out of his way; Hitler (I met him once when he was in a fiendish temper) was a vulgarian who did not care tuppence for his neighbour, and had an insatiable appetite for expansion; while Stalin harnessed the secret police and the armed forces behind Communist doctrine, which authorized subversion and, where necessary, force to achieve a political aim.

Such dictators place a Christian democracy in a cruel dilemma. We are instructed by our religion to respect our neighbour, and that the meek will inherit the earth. No one will contest that this is an attractive philosophy, and that it is morally meritorious and ethically right, but how ought a Christian to interpret those precepts in the face of overbearing power? There are some – and they are sincere people – who will hold that it is enough to march under the banner of 'Peace'.

In the thirties we had the Peace Pledge Union. Their propaganda was so morally infectious that it delayed one Prime Minister from going to the country and fighting an Election on a platform of re-armament, and inhibited him even when he had obtained the mandate to go ahead.

You will probably have heard of the motion in the Oxford Union which declared that the young would no longer fight for King and Country. All very democratic and plausibly Christian, but Hitler got the message, and we now know that Britain's apparent pacifism encouraged him to discount the official warnings that Britain would fight.

Our pacifist version of today is the Campaign for Nuclear Disarmament which has some Bishops and many Churchmen in its ranks. They know that the Russian Communist is not affected by any moral consideration, but they still preach, with apparent conviction that, given a unilateral lead on disarmament, the Kremlin will follow suit. The very last thing your generation wants is a nuclear war, and the young are tempted to approve this simple reasoning, as were the generation who died forty years ago.

I will tell you in a later letter that over twenty-five years of dealing with Russia's leaders I have not seen a shred of evidence that they can be disarmed by example.

Of course a Christian democracy has no option but to deal in conciliation – to take any other course would be to be untrue to all its ideals.

What attitude, however, does a Christian society take when the crunch comes and everything, including its religion, is in imminent danger of forcible take-over by alien arms and an alien doctrine? Would you rather be Red or Dead? This unfortunately is even now no academic question, as the Afghans, or the Boatpeople of South-East Asia, or the Poles will testify.

I am tempted here to continue with the story of Lenin and the Russian revolution, and how Stalin converted it into an instrument of naked power, but I think I will postpone that tale in favour of a look at the twenties and thirties when, having put one terrible conflict behind us, Christian men and women of good will pledged themselves to outlaw war.

Let us see how they fared.

Letter Three

Towards the end of last week's letter I asked the somewhat rhetorical question whether we could find an answer to the intolerable poser 'Would you rather be Red than Dead?' I am going to approach the problem obliquely for reasons which, if you have the patience to read to the end, I hope will seem to be good.

You will remember that I wrote that Sir Edward Grey could not think of any short-comings in his negotiations to try and avert the catastrophe of 1914, but for one nagging doubt. Would the Kaiser have attacked if, well in advance, he had been given the most unequivocal warning that Britain would certainly fight?

Similarly when Hitler was showing signs of following in the Kaiser's footsteps, would he have moved his troops into the Rhineland, if Britain and France had convinced him in advance that if he went ahead with the idea the German troops would be ejected by force?

That, of course, could be argued until the

cows come home, but that is not my immediate point. The point is that two lots of peace-makers dealing with two arrogant bullies came to the conclusion that the only thing which could have deterred them from their evil intentions was the knowledge that they would be faced with superior force, and with probable defeat.

Keep that in mind while I introduce you to the personalities who were to strain every nerve to find ways of living with a resurgent Germany, but ended up with Hitler's war.

The principals, as I have indicated, were Stanley Baldwin, Winston Churchill and Neville Chamberlain, and I think I must add Ramsay Macdonald who played a transient but significant rôle.

You will recall the backcloth – a British people sickened by war; determined out of its ashes to build, in Lloyd George's picturesque phrase 'a land fit for heroes to live in'; and buoyed up by hope and trust in the League of Nations to provide their security.

I think I can best convey the extraordinary degree to which this theme gripped the whole country by an illustration from Winston Churchill's years at the Treasury. He had made his reputation as a student of war, and in particular as the Minister responsible for the Navy, and yet as

Chancellor of the Exchequer between 1924 and 1929 he cut the finances of his beloved Services to the bone; so harshly indeed that the Chiefs of Staff threatened to resign because they considered that the levels of forces and weaponry were being reduced below the margin of safety.

Once before in the government of Mr Asquith Churchill had vetoed the building of eight dreadnoughts. Then there were technical pros and cons, but on this occasion the only conclusion which is at all convincing is that he insisted on the cuts because of his belief that for the future the League of Nations would provide collective security against aggression from any quarter.

There was, too, a curious device adopted by the 1924–29 Government of which Churchill was a member, which was known as the 'No war for 10 years rule'. There was to be a yearly rolling review of Britain's military needs in relation to the world security situation, and, according to the findings, our levels of forces would be adapted to meet the situation. The 'rule' was still in operation in 1932, and nothing had been done in the way of re-armament!

I recall these facts to give you some idea of how completely everyone was caught up in the great expectation that the League of Nations would guarantee peace.

With the benefit of hindsight we can recognize that with America opting for isolation, and with Russia crippled by the aftermath of revolution, the hopes of a guaranteed peace were optimistic, but then the overwhelming mood was that the political barometer was set fair for harmonious international relations. The lesson of war had not been learned.

Churchill, as we shall see, was the first to prick the balloon of general euphoria, and his warnings of the militarist revival in Germany became more and more urgent, but as late as 1932 even he was still able to say in an interview in New York, 'I do not believe we shall see another war in our lifetime.' It was seven years ahead.

I expect you have seen in the Provost's Lodge at Eton the striking portraits of the great statesmen of the 18th and 19th centuries, which were painted when they were boys in the school. These pictures first brought home to me that these men who were just facts in the history books were people like us.

You won't find pictures there of Churchill or Baldwin (they were both Harrovians!) so I thought I might try a pen–sketch of those two, and of Ramsay Macdonald and Neville Chamberlain, who were the leading actors on the stage as we approached Hitler's war.

Stanley Baldwin was a sterling character. An industrialist who had given half his considerable fortune to the nation in 1914 to help the war effort. He was conspicuously – but by no means narrowly – a patriot. He had extraordinarily acute political antennae which enabled him to sense and to interpret the public mood almost before the people themselves were aware of it. These skills he employed with impressive success over ten years. His sense of timing in the General Strike of 1926 was immaculate, while in the constitutional crisis involving the Abdication of King Edward VIII he acted with great intuition, sensitivity and absolute authority.

He found himself in 1935 Prime Minister in a Parliament where the massive majority were Conservatives, with the Socialists reduced to around fifty left-wing members. These demoralized men he handled with a velvet glove and led them along the constitutional path of a democratic opposition. The historians will mark that as his great contribution to the British political scene. On occasions he could show conspicuous political courage, but he preferred to get his way by stealth.

Baldwin had one weakness. He was ill at ease with foreigners, and used to go so far as to contrive that he need not sit next to them at meals!

What did he look like? Short and broad in figure and face, he had some curious mannerisms in the House of Commons. He would first make excruciating faces, and then smack kisses on the Order Paper as though he was starved of affection! – he wasn't, as he was a popular and successful Prime Minister.

Ramsay Macdonald, the architect of the Socialist Party, and its first Prime Minister, came into the limelight when the National Government was formed to cope with the economic and financial crisis of 1931. But he was much more than a figurehead of convenience. With strong leanings towards pacifism he had made himself a considerable reputation in international circles as a peace-maker. With a fine physical presence, and the authentic accent of the Highland Scot he was in his prime a compelling platform orator.

Late in his political career he succumbed to the flattery of being lionized by some of the Conservative hostesses of London, and lost caste with his Socialist companions, but on any count national or international, he was a personality in his own right.

I am going to put the pictures of Churchill and Chamberlain side by side, so that you can look easily from one to the other, for they were a total contrast, and not least in appearance.

If you can imagine a cross between a pink, chubby, cherubic baby, and a bulldog which hunches its shoulders and growls – that is Churchill.

He was gregarious in the company he enjoyed. Chamberlain was by comparison a spare corvine figure, economical in speech and humour and select to the point of fastidiousness in his choice of friends.

Churchill was the ebullient extrovert. Everything about him – his habits, his hobbies, his language, his politics – was vivid.

Chamberlain was shy and reserved, shirking the limelight, content with efficiency for its own reward, guided in all he did by reason. Everything about him was in shades of grey.

Churchill was ever ready to gamble with fortune. Chamberlain was the trustee – careful to conserve.

During the 1924–29 Parliament they exchanged frequent notes with each other. From them it is clear that, while they respected each other's admirable qualities, Churchill saw Chamberlain as cautious and unimaginative, while Chamberlain saw Churchill as temperamentally and incurably erratic.

Churchill's emotions were public property – Chamberlain's controlled and private. Churchill was counselled by instinct, Chamberlain by facts.

I could continue endlessly, but you are probably beginning to get a good idea of these two distinguished personalities.

Always there is contrast, and the result is two characters, both of whom commanded great respect from the onlookers, but who in contact with each other were always more likely to irritate than to understand. Their one point of agreement was that they would rather be Dead than Red.

To indulge in 'might-have-beens' is always an unprofitable exercise, but what misery we could have been spared if in good time the genius and the flair of the one could have been harnessed to the intellectual discipline and the method of the other!

Next week we will follow their fortunes as they took over the stage, and the political drama came to its climax in war.

PS I must not give you the impression that Neville Chamberlain was an unattractive personality. He was a good naturalist – a really knowledgeable observer of birds, butterflies and animals. He liked his fishing and shooting, and was skilled at them. He was fond too of music.

None of this, however, was seen by the public, and his talents and attractions were kept for only a few intimate friends. That was his deliberate choice.

Letter Four

There are several separate threads which have to be woven together if the political situation throughout the thirties is to become clear.

The first clue comes from the word 'erratic' which you may remember I put into Chamberlain's mouth as applying to Churchill. There were in fact a lot of people who would have concurred with that assessment.

A number of elder Conservatives had blamed him for the spectacular failure of the Gallipoli expedition in the war, and even more had criticized his romantic support of the White Russian military campaign to try and reverse the course of the Communist revolution.

A different group was opposed to his colourful advocacy of a return to the Gold Standard, while virtually the whole of the Socialist party wrote him off because of his known and entrenched opposition to independence for the continent of India. No one questioned his energy or his talents, or his brilliance, but doubts increased as to his judgement.

It is difficult to see how Ramsay Macdonald could have included him in the National Government of 1931, and at the same time brought with him J. H. Thomas, Philip Snowden, Sir Herbert Samuel, Lord Sankey and others who were necessary to give to it a semblance of genuine coalition. Yet the omission was grievous, for in isolation Churchill ceased to be in daily contact with Conservative Ministers. He could no longer inspire the Cabinet with his imagination, and they could not restrain his impetuosity.

Churchill, therefore, became something of a loner, and this was confirmed by the crisis which arose over the abdication of King Edward VIII. His loyalty to a personal friend was understood, but his championship of the King's marriage to an American divorcée was seen by a great majority of the British people as allowing his private feelings to over-ride his responsibility as a Member of Parliament and statesman on an issue of prime constitutional importance to the country.

Once more the fault was laid at the door of his judgement. That was tragic, for this crisis came at a time when he might have been brought back into the Government and when, in the Cabinet, he could have proved that his information about

German re-armament was right, in which case
action to meet the threat would have been bound
to follow.

The Government, first under Ramsay Macdonald's leadership and then under Baldwin's,
had two chances to follow Churchill's lead and
to re-arm. The first was when the official information about the rate of expansion of the German
air-force was proved to be wrong, and the second
when, having asked for a mandate for re-armament in the General Election of 1935, the country
backed Baldwin's request with a decisive
majority.

You will remember that he had been greatly
affected by the campaign of the Peace Pledge
Union and the eleven million people who
signed it, and even now he was reluctant to
change course abruptly. He calculated that there
was still time to reach a *modus vivendi* with
Germany which would avoid war, and he felt
that rapid re-armament could prejudice that
prospect.

It was in fact Neville Chamberlain, the
'appeaser' and Lord Swinton, who pushed ahead
with the two military projects which were
authorized, which were the production of the
aeroplanes 'Hurricane' and 'Spitfire'.

Their action was late, and only just in time as

it proved to save the country in the Battle of Britain. Too little credit has been given to these two for their foresight.

Neither Baldwin nor Chamberlain nor a great many more comprehended the vast revolution in industry which it would require to service the forces overseas through a long war.

With the benefit of hindsight it is clear that Churchill was right, and that we ought to have begun massive and serious re-armament at the latest by 1936. It is just possible that had we done so the evidence of Britain's strength might have deterred Hitler from war.

But there is one myth about this period which was, and perhaps still is, widely held, and that is that the Foreign Office was against the Conservative Government's policy of trying to find a negotiated settlement which could deflect Hitler from war. That was said to be particularly true of Sir Robert Vansittart and Mr Ralph Wigram who were the Permanent officials at the top.

That simply was not so. The British Ambassadors in Berlin were continually consulted as to the possibilities of détente. Anthony Eden in 1934 – and he was no friend of dictators – felt able to tell Mussolini that in his opinion Hitler seemed to be sincere in desiring a disarmament convention, and there was in fact an agreement

signed which limited the German navy to 35%
of the strength of the British fleet.

The best evidence, however, that Ministers
and officials were working harmoniously, and
were agreed on the objective, is given in a docu-
ment prepared in 1937 by Sir Orme Sargent, a
senior Foreign Office official, for circulation to
the Cabinet.

It read as follows:

'The fundamental idea, is of course, that the
ex-allied Powers should come to terms with
Germany, in order to remove grievances by
friendly arrangement, and the process of
give and take, before Germany again takes
the law into her own hands. This is the only
constructive policy open to Europe.

The alternative policy of drift and en-
circlement are avowedly policies of nega-
tion and despair. There will in this Memor-
andum be no suggestion that the policy
should be abandoned.'

Chamberlain would have approved every
word of it. His critics' aim, however, was not so
much directed at conciliation, for if at all possible
a *modus vivendi* with Germany had to be found,
but at those who failed to recognize that the best

chance that it would succeed lay in simultaneously mobilizing military power designed to deter.

To seek peace by increasing arms is an argument against which the tolerant peoples of a democracy instinctively revolt. We do so now when the Russians pose a similar challenge, but in those days we were not so hardened in the ways of the aggressor.

Baldwin and Chamberlain postponed again and again the full mobilization of the nation's strength in the hope of peace by example. Hitler, coldly calculating British and French weakness, planned his war.

Letter Five

In my last letter I used up all my time and space discussing the dilemma which is posed between what would seem to be the conflicting policies of conciliation and re-armament. That, if I keep up this correspondence, will I fear be a lasting theme, but for the moment I have something to say about luck in politics, which is very relevant to the period of which I am writing.

Just at the time when the politicians of Britain and France ought to have been concentrating on Hitler and his doings, there were two diversions which can only have been designed by some malicious devil. One was Italy's invasion of Abyssinia, and the other the Spanish Civil War. Each in its different way was a disaster.

The roots of the Italian monarchy, which were not very deep, had been loosened in the Kaiser's war, and by the economic aftermath, and it was no great surprise when, from the social and economic plight of the country, a para-military dictatorship took over.

Mussolini to look at was almost totally square, square body, square face and square head which incidentally was quite bald, and to make up for his lack of inches he walked with his chin tilted in the air. But although he was an upstart Dictator he had made quite a good beginning when he took over power. He identified himself with the desire of the majority of Italians for law and order, and he proceeded with a course of general spring-cleaning which was long overdue. New and impressive buildings sprang up; litter was collected; the trains ran more nearly to time and so on; but then Mussolini was bitten by the bug of power, and he launched an attack on Abyssinia to protect, as he claimed, long-standing Italian interests in that country and that part of Africa.

The supporters of the League of Nations and collective security had already seen Japan invade Chinese territory, but that aggression was far away, and even America, the guardian of the Pacific Ocean, had done nothing but protest with words. The United States was not a member of the League.

Here, however, was something very different, a European country, Italy, bound by the terms of the covenant, without notice or consultation attacking a backward and almost defenceless

African territory. If ever there was to be an obligation on the membership of the League to take collective action to prevent the Italian forces from reaching their target this was it.

On paper this was about as easy a test case for the League of Nations as could have been designed, and the British Government was unanimous that collective opposition to Italy should be mobilized, and Sir Samuel Hoare, the Foreign Secretary, was instructed to give a lead. This he did with some powerful speeches at international gatherings, only to have to report after all his exhortations that he could not extract the promise of 'a ship, a machine or a gun'. Military sanctions therefore were a flop.

There was another possibility. Oil was necessary if Italy was to transport her troops to Egypt and then to Abyssinia by sea, and oil could be embargoed and blockaded. That course seemed to be promising, and Chamberlain for one was strongly in favour of it. Then the snag arose. No one would commit themselves unless all did so, and that unanimity proved to be impossible to achieve.

You will at once see the significance of this failure. The hopes which in Britain had for many years been firmly anchored on the League to prevent war, had been shattered, and by a minor Dictator and a lesser power, while all the time Hitler was looking on. You can imagine the disillusion which followed that collapse of faith and hope.

There was nothing for it then if Mussolini was not to rebound into Hitler's arms, but to try and extract from the wreckage a negotiated settlement to which the Italian dictator and the Emperor of Abyssinia would both subscribe.

The French were particularly keen on a deal, and Monsieur Laval, their Foreign Minister, was their representative in quadrilateral talks – Britain, France, Italy and Abyssinia – the aims of which were to settle the particular dispute and to serve as a prelude to a comprehensive settlement of all Europe's problems. After hard and secret diplomatic bargaining the bones of an agreement appeared which seemed to be generally acceptable. It involved a transfer of part of the Ogaden to Italy – an area of Abyssinia which was of little use to the Emperor.

Then the leak came. Whether or not Laval, who had the reputation of being a slick operator, engineered it in order to put pressure on the other negotiators to agree was never proved, but at once in the British Parliament the fat was in the fire.

The Foreign Secretary, Sir Samuel Hoare, was

judged at best to have been duped by the French, and at worst to have been party to a shady transaction to sell the Emperor down the river. Here again the imp of luck took a hand. Sir Samuel at the time was on holiday in Switzerland, and had fallen on the ice and damaged his arm and broken his nose. Never overburdened with humour he was reported as saying that he had returned in haste, even though it meant 'leaving behind Lady Maud and the luggage', so all-in-all he met a House of Commons which was in a mood to ridicule and condemn.

His defence of his collaborations with Laval was full-blooded, but it did not prevail, and he had to resign. The resignation of a Foreign Secretary and a public reversal of his policy is a traumatic event in politics – you remember that of Lord Carrington – and the Government was badly scarred. Lloyd George, I remember, turning the dagger in the wound, saying in relation to the Government's past championship of the League: 'They have borne aloft a torch for all the world to see, and now it has been quenched with a "hiss" '. You can scarcely imagine the venom in the word, and I can still feel the physical recoil as the old white-headed cobra poised for the strike!

Nevertheless, the historians are likely to

conclude that the penchant of the British for the under-dog (in this case an Emperor) blinded the nation to the advantage of a piece of real politics which could have brought considerable gains to Britain and to Europe.

Chamberlain, who was nothing if not a realist, was particularly disappointed by the Abyssinian fiasco, but he did not despair of the possibility of diverting Mussolini from the Berlin axis back into the allied fold. He therefore cultivated him, using as his go-between his sister-in-law, the widow of his half-brother Austen. Eden, the Foreign Secretary, resented the fact that he kept this correspondence private (and he had a point of propriety), but on the merits it ought to be remembered that in the event Italy did not answer Hitler's summons to arms until the military collapse of France presented an irresistible temptation to Mussolini's cupidity. That Italy might never have gone to war but for that unforeseen débâcle is one of the haunting 'ifs' of history.

Italy was also a prime mover in the other accidental disaster which I mentioned – the Spanish Civil War.

You must be asking yourself how it was that a domestic row in Spain had such an impact on the Governments of Britain and France, and indeed further afield.

The reason was that Europe was beginning to divide on ideologies; Socialism and Communism for those who favoured the social and economic doctrine of Karl Marx, and Capitalism for those who were traditionally and conservatively inclined.

In Spain's Civil War an International Brigade was recruited and fought for the Left, while General Franco was supported by extremists on the Right, and many from European countries volunteered for the ranks of one or the other. Communist Russia sent advisers and arms to the one side, and Fascist Italy did the same for the other.

The French really had something to worry about, as Hitler's sympathies lay with Franco, and had the two joined forces they would have been in the middle of a most unsavoury sandwich.

Monsieur Blum, the colourful Socialist head of the government known as the Front Populaire because it was allied to the Communists, was their Prime Minister. He settled on an ingenious device of 'non-alignment' which meant that, however many volunteers crossed the Spanish frontier, 'official' France would keep out of the fight, and supply neither men nor arms. The British Government concurred and followed suit.

The result was that the Socialists in the British Parliament harried the Government week in and week out against a posture of neutrality while an embryo Dictator in General Franco was killing and wounding their Spanish comrades. To add fuel to the flames there were casualties among the British volunteers, some of whom returned with lurid tales of cruelties inflicted which were all too true as each side matched the other with atrocities.

The Parliamentary assault was met with great skill by Sir Anthony Eden and R. A. Butler, but they could never satisfy – only stone-wall.

The ordeal lasted two years and more, and the fury of the Left never abated. In all the years I was in Parliament (and that included the Suez crisis) I never saw tempers so naked and raw.

It is no exaggeration to say that this prolonged and smouldering controversy was catastrophic.

In Britain the Government was trying to bring about a consensus on re-armament in the face of an increasing peril from Germany, while internationally both France and Britain were seeking a comprehensive settlement of Europe's complicated problems. The tragedy of it was that at this critical time Hitler, who had an acute political nose, kept a low profile, completing his plans for war, while the British and French were looking the other way.

My experience of politics is that things seldom turn out in the way anticipated, but I think you will agree that some evil genius was at work when he pulled out of his box of political tricks both Abyssinia and the Spanish Civil War.

Letter Six

I hope I have been able to give you some idea of the inter-reaction between the people and the events of these extraordinary years – of how the good and the well-meaning and the peaceful were slowly and painfully being brought up against the hard reality that violence and the lust for power were still facts of life, and of how in Britain rapid re-armament was increasingly associated with Churchill, and caution and conciliation with Chamberlain.

You are probably asking yourself why, when the German military machine was becoming so obviously strong, and when Hitler's declamatory speeches were more strident every day, Chamberlain hesitated to step up the pace of re-armament?

He had several reasons for not doing so.

He had been much affected by the economic collapse of 1931, and he was afraid that the steeply rising costs which were bound to accompany a massive re-armament programme would reverse the economic recovery which five years of prudent finance had so hardly won.

All Chancellors of the Exchequer look askance at unproductive expenditure on the Armed Forces. New aeroplanes for the Royal Air Force, and some modest increases for the other two Services were as much as he felt was consistent with good financial stewardship. He looked upon himself in that particular office as Trustee for the value of money.

I will come to the state of public opinion in Britain later in this letter, but Chamberlain as Prime Minister in 1938 had also to consider the attitude of the Dominions. The assent of Australia, New Zealand and Canada at the least would be necessary before war could be declared, and at that time none of the leaders of those countries was persuaded that the limits of negotiation had been reached. Any British Prime Minister had to be sure of their approval and active backing.

Chamberlain had other less tangible but valid reasons for trying to win time in which he might divert Hitler from his warlike intentions. He had no confidence in France as a reliable ally. The French were the people most affected by the German remilitarization of the Rhineland, but they had shown no sign of wanting to intervene.

They were the country which had the Treaty obligation to go to the defence of the Czechs should they be the target for aggression, but they continually prevaricated on the issue.

In this assessment of the French Chamberlain and Churchill were poles apart. Churchill was a Francophile to the emotional point where France could do no wrong. All his strategic plans in relation to a European war were based on the assumption of the invincibility of the French army, and he would listen to no criticism of it. He was, of course, tragically wrong in his judgement, and when we come to the Munich agreement I will allow myself to speculate as to whether he would have been so contemptuous and condemnatory of it if he had appreciated the true state of the French forces and of French morale.

However that may be there is one more consideration which influenced Chamberlain profoundly in his search for more time. It was his conviction that, should the countries of Central Europe tear themselves apart, the sole beneficiary would be Communist Russia. He found it difficult to believe that Hitler, who hated the Russians, could be so blind as to ignore that obvious danger which overhung Germany.

Chamberlain was right about the French, and

in the longer run he was right about the Russians; so where was he wrong?

If a country is to go to war the people must be led to consensus and unity. That would have been hard enough for a Baldwin, who was a natural builder of political bridges, but for Neville Chamberlain it was much more difficult. He could not conceal his intellectual contempt for the Socialist Opposition in Parliament, and in particular for their pacifism, and in his speeches it showed. He would sting and sting again, and then strike for the kill. He was a skilled and merciless debater, and the Labour benches were routed over and over again. That was the basic reason why the Socialist leaders refused to come into a coalition under his leadership, even after he had declared war on behalf of the nation.

However I think that the real mistake which Chamberlain made was in persuading himself that where neither concessions nor persuasion nor power had changed Hitler's mind, that his own reasonable approach could do so. That is how we arrived at a situation in which all that stood between the Western democracies and the German dictator was the reason, the persistence and the courage of one man.

If blame is to be allocated where should it lie? I would answer that question like this:

On the slogan adopted after the 1914–18 war that this had been the 'war to end all wars', which derived from the horror of the experience, rather than a sober strategic calculation of dangers present and impending.

On the depth of the British people's conviction that the League of Nations would provide a substitute for national defence.

On the reduction in the mid-ninteen twenties of the armed forces below the level of safety which encouraged that belief.

On the misleading 'No war for ten years rule'.

On the inability of the European members of the League of Nations to prevent Italy's invasion of Abyssinia.

On the failure of the French and the British to warn Hitler that the remilitarization of the Rhineland would be resisted by force.

On the official mis-information conveyed to the British Government as to the real strength of the German air-force.

On Baldwin's reluctance to take advantage of the 1935 General Election to go for serious re-armament.

On the obsession of the French and the British with the Spanish Civil War.

On Chamberlain's tenacious belief, in spite of

the evidence of fact, that reason and example would influence a Dictator dedicated to the use of military power.

That is quite a catalogue, stretching over a long time.

We shall shortly see how the odium for 'appeasement' was to concentrate on the head of Chamberlain, but blame – if blame there is to be – should be spread over many more people and over many more years.

Letter Seven

As we came into the year 1938 tensions in Europe were rising as Hitler's declarations and speeches became more and more strident, and his ambitions increased. The crisis, which arose out of his demands on Czecho-Slovakia and the drama of the Munich meeting was to be played out in the House of Commons, so I will try to give you a picture of some of the people there, and of the mood they were in.

The bare statistics are these. The Conservatives, with a majority of 200 and more over all parties; the Liberals with their ranks greatly depleted when compared with earlier times; the Socialists considerably recovered from the electoral débâcle of 1931, and just able to sustain a working Opposition, and the four Clydesiders, Maxton, McGovern, Campbell Steven, and Wheatley who were in terms of dialectics the most effective debaters of the lot.

Let me take the parties, in their reverse order of influence.

Maxton was the laziest of revolutionaries. He would talk cricket by the hour, and you cannot do that and deal in violence! Of the others who formed the I.L.P. Campbell Steven and Wheatley were the brains; and McGovern the brawn. He was later to become a muscular Christian, strongly opposed to the doctrines of Karl Marx. You can wash these four out of your calculations in the balance of Parliamentary power. They provided intellectual spice and much entertainment, but they had no influence on events.

In the early twenties the Liberal Party, even though it had been weakened by the fight between Lloyd George and Asquith, was still a recognizable unit, but by 1931, when Sir John Simon, Sir Godfrey Collins, Sir Herbert Samuel and Sir Archibald Sinclair all crossed the floor to serve in the National Government, they had lost their distinct identity.

Simon had one of the keenest legal brains in the country, (he had only to declare the General Strike of 1926 illegal for it to collapse like a house of cards), but he was a cool and detached and somewhat inhuman figure and never attracted a following.

Samuel was the philosopher of Liberalism. He was competent and reliable and a good Home Secretary; he made speeches of such immaculate grammar that they almost always lost their impact and message.

Samuel and Sinclair returned to the Liberal benches unable to stomach any dilution of Free Trade, although the process of extracting them from the National Government was described as 'like pulling kittens by their tails from a jug of cream', and it was not long before all these 'deserters' began to lose influence. Coalitions soon outlive the purpose for which they are assembled.

There was a rump of pure Liberals left with Clement Davies, and Miss Megan Lloyd George, fighting for political survival, but they did not hold the attention of the House. Megan Lloyd George tried to be a ball of fire, but she could not hold a candle to her father, and was anyhow too gentle and nice to carry through her self-appointed rôle.

So once again you may dismiss both species of Liberals, for they had a negligible influence on the unfolding political scene.

The Socialist Parliamentary Party, you will remember, had been virtually annihilated in 1931, and since then their partial recovery had been very pedestrian. By 1936 there were some new members who were beginning to make their mark. One was Clement Attlee, later of course to be Prime Minister. His position in Parliament was due to the fact that he was one of the few Socialists who had survived the 1931 election. For a long time he was under-estimated. Someone once said to Churchill 'You must admit that there are good points about Clem.' To which he answered, 'Take a grub and feed it on royal jelly, and it will become a Queen Bee!'

Of all the politicians I have known Attlee used the fewest words. A colleague, after a conversation with him, turned politely at the door and said, 'Is there anything more I can do for you?' 'Yes, go,' was the uncompromising reply. To another who asked if he might be told why he was being sacked, he said, 'Because you are not up to the job.'

Attlee and Greenwood were the most effective critics of the Government's foreign policy, but they did not add up to much.

Aneurin Bevan was there, but had not graduated beyond domestic politics; while Ernest Bevin who was not in Parliament at the time, was still occupied with Trade Union business.

The official Opposition in Parliament then was still weak and ineffective. The result was that the direction and control of events lay with the Conservative Parliamentary party, and the Government, which with Baldwin having retired, and the restraints of coalition fading, had lined up with enthusiasm behind Neville Chamberlain.

Soon after his election as Leader of the Party and his appointment as Prime Minister, he had explained his foreign policy to the back-benchers. He told them plainly that he might have come on the scene too late to stop a war with Germany, but that he still hoped to be able to detach Italy from the Berlin axis. He did not in that speech say very much about re-armament, but he was known to have approved the strengthening of the Air Force. His followers were therefore fully aware of his intentions, and they knew too that Chamberlain and Eden had expressed relief that the era of Baldwin's drift in foreign policy had come to an end, and that they welcomed the opportunity to work with each other. So far so good.

In my next letter I will try and explain to you how it was that things began to go sour between the Prime Minister and his Foreign Secretary; but in the meantime let me give you the form of some of the younger Conservatives who were also to be caught up in the traumatic events to come.

Anthony Eden and R. A. Butler were the most prominent, and each had already proved himself under political fire in Parliament.

Eden, trained under Austen Chamberlain, was the accomplished diplomat, popular at home and patient, persuasive and flexible in his contacts with foreign statesmen. He had an almost unfair ration of charm, and if occasionally there appeared a touch of vanity there was certainly a lot which could be put to his credit while still a young man.

Butler, by contrast, was the intellectual backroom boy who was invaluable to the Party as an originator of policy. He had also proved his Parliamentary ability in the conduct of the India Independence Bill through the House, and in his tough defence of the Government's policy of non-intervention during the Spanish Civil War.

Lord Cranborne was there, the latest of the line of Cecils who had given service to the country since the time of Queen Elizabeth I. He had an extensive vocabulary, a ready wit, and an agile mind. He was to prove like other members of his family, a successful Minister, but a ready resigner, and this slightly reduced his influence.

Oliver Stanley, (a younger son of Lord Derby), Duff Cooper and Walter Elliot were a trio of intellectual excellence. The first would sum up a complicated debate, and apparently the only aid he required was a succession of 'doodles'. The second had an astonishing photographic memory to the point where he once introduced the Army estimates in a speech of over two hours without a single note. The third, a Scotsman, was possessed of remarkable versatility, and filled a succession of high offices with great distinction.

Then there was Captain Harry Crookshank, whose debating skill and sense of the ridiculous and command of procedure could tie the Socialist opposition into knots of frustration.

So you will see that there was plenty of talent there, and independence of mind. They were by no means 'yes men'.

As Churchill stepped up his campaign against the Government for failing to re-arm at speed, and as Eden began to cavil at Chamberlain's intervention in foreign policy with its scant consultation with the Foreign Office, these influential younger Conservatives found their allegiance to be strained.

Eden, Cranborne, Duff Cooper and others leaned towards Churchill; Butler, Stanley, Crookshank and Elliot remained with Chamberlain; while among others there was uncertainty and deep unease. Groups were formed (the Eden lot were called 'the glamour boys') and tempers became frayed.

My particular friend, J. P. L. Thomas, was Parliamentary Private Secretary to Eden, as I was to Chamberlain, and between us we tried to reconcile our chiefs to each other. It was not easy. Eden was temperamental, and lived on his nerves; while Chamberlain's reaction to a crisis of personal relations was an icy and forbidding calm. Our efforts to build bridges were not conspicuously successful. On the last occasion that I staged a meeting, Eden had a streaming cold, and as he came into the room Chamberlain looked up and told him to go and take two aspirins, and to come back in the morning when he would make more sense! That sounds petty, but politics are about people, and in this case the substance of their differences ran deep.

How deep I can illustrate by bringing forward in time Churchill's verdict on Chamberlain and on the Government at the time of Munich.

'Five futile years of good intentions; five years of eager search for the line of least resistance; five years of uninterrupted defeat of British power; five years of neglecting the air defences. We have been reduced these five years from a position so over-whelming and so unchallengeable . . .'

Next week I will try and answer the question 'Was it really as bad as that?'

Letter Eight

Don't be bored if I start this letter by reminding you that it would have been very much better if re-armament had begun in earnest in 1935, or at latest in 1936.

Of course we now know that Hitler was an evil man, who wished to get his way by force rather than by negotiation, so it is probable that earlier action by Britain would not have deterred him from invading the Low Countries, and launching an attack on France, but that is no excuse for not taking any precaution which might have convinced him that the risk of war was too high. That opportunity had been missed, and by 1938 the area of diplomatic manoeuvre open to Chamberlain had been very much narrowed, and the time-scale in which to find a settlement had been much curtailed.

Essentially the British Government was faced with a situation in which it had to gain time. Time for diplomacy to work, and time for the armaments from the production lines to reach the forces.

When Hitler threatened to take over the Sudetenland of Czecho-Slovakia even this tight time-table was cut. So urgent and challenging did Chamberlain judge this matter to be that he decided to meet Hitler face to face in order to try and convince him of the real dangers of war if he persisted in his demands, and of the fateful consequence for Europe if Britain and France and Germany were to fight.

For a Prime Minister to jump into an aeroplane and meet another Head of State would not now raise an eyebrow, but at that time statesmen did not fly to meet each other, and Chamberlain had never flown before. So his journey to Berchtesgarten was a novel, daring, spectacular and moving event.

At the meeting one problem to be explored was the possibility of plebiscite in which the people of the Sudetenland would vote and determine their own destiny. After a short discussion Chamberlain left Hitler to consider the details of such an exercise, while he in turn went home to consult the British Cabinet. His approach and his handling of his talks with Hitler were then approved by the whole Cabinet.

After a few days he returned to see Hitler, this time at Godesberg, where he was met by a new and unacceptable demand that German troops should enter Czecho-Slovakia in advance of the result of the plebiscite being known. Chamberlain rejected that proposition and left expecting war. Before leaving, however, he had thrown to Hitler a life-line which was the possibility of a Four-Power meeting between Britain and France, Germany and Italy before any irrevocable action was taken. Again his conduct of those proceedings was approved by the Cabinet, which included Duff Cooper.

In a message which arrived into my hands in the very last seconds of Chamberlain's speech to the House of Commons summing up the recent events, Hitler agreed to attend. Until that moment everyone in the Chamber had concluded that we were heading straight for war. The scene was high drama as the whole House rose in relief and acclaim. At the very least the Prime Minister single-handed had gained time.

The question then turned on the kind and the degree of sacrifice which the French and British would require from the Czechs to avert the catastrophe of immediate war. The Treaty which emerged from the discussion included self-determination for the Sudetens, and a Czecho-Slovakia with new boundaries to be safeguarded by international guarantee. The risks in such a programme had to be weighed against the imminence and impact of war. The conclusion reached by the British and French was that the settlement should be endorsed. It was that decision which led to Churchill's bitter denunciation which I have already quoted to you.

It was possible to argue the case that Czecho-Slovakia would have been better off embraced in a comprehensive settlement for Europe than if she had remained a target of continued German subversion, but that question became academic as Hitler within months lost all his self-control and invaded and took over the whole country.

The sacrifice of the Czechs was the gravamen of the charge of dishonourable appeasement, to which was added the accusation of writing off the military value of the Czech army.

Were these charges valid?

A Prime Minister is above all the trustee of the security of his own country, and Chamberlain in that context had once said that for the greater good it might be necessary in Britain's interest to do something which in normal circumstances he would not wish to do. In this case the imperative was to gain time.

As to the military value of the Czech army, that had been completely neutralized by the Austrian Anschluss, and it would have been surrounded and annihilated in a matter of weeks.

In fact, during those days, this was virtually confirmed by Dr Benes, who told the late Professor Harold Temperley that Bohemia could not have lasted more than three weeks. I think this assessment was optimistic even for the whole of Czecho-Slovakia.

There was another consideration very much in Chamberlain's mind, and that was the unreliability of the French. Here he was right.

While Churchill, as we have seen, was properly urging substantial increases of armaments, all his strategic assessments were based on the invincibility of the French army. He was so passionate a Francophile that he refused to contemplate any weakness in their political will, or in their military machine. In his assessment of Germany's strength he was totally right, and in his estimate of the French completely wrong.

Could a Prime Minister, responsible for his country's survival, and aware of its weakness and lack of preparation, have chosen to risk an immediate war?

Chamberlain, if Churchill had won his case on re-armament in 1936, would not have arrived at Munich with so few cards in his hand, but the historians may well judge that whatever the previous errors Chamberlain was right at that moment to play for time, and that any other

Prime Minister would have had to do the same.

I am going to stick out my neck and say that the British Government was wrong about rearmament and that Chamberlain was right at Munich.

Was Chamberlain culpably gullible? In any conversations I had with him he showed no sign of having been duped. He had no illusions about Hitler's character, and looked upon him as boorish and crude, and ruthless in his use of his power.

However on Chamberlain's public performance it is understandable that many people concluded that he had been manipulated and fooled.

The first piece of evidence which was quoted in support of this thesis was the piece of paper which he displayed at Northolt Airport which declared that in future any disputes between Britain and Germany would be settled by peaceful means. The decision to give publicity to Hitler's signature to that declaration was deliberate. Chamberlain argued that if Hitler kept his word well and good, and if he broke it he would be guilty before the world of having torn up one more solemn promise. In that case Chamberlain knew exactly what he was doing.

But what about the words spoken from the window of Downing Street, when he claimed that he had brought back from Germany 'Peace with Honour'?

The Munich agreement might perhaps be justified as unavoidable or as expedient, but few if any would have linked it with honour. I have written elsewhere of this episode on our return to London which I witnessed as we went up the stairs in Downing Street, but you may not have read of it so I will repeat it now.

In the jostling of a packed crowd on the stairs in No. 10 I heard someone, whose identity I could not fix, say to Chamberlain, 'Neville, go to the window and repeat the historic words, "Peace with honour"'. His response was short – even curt. 'No, I do not do that kind of thing.'

That was the authentic Chamberlain. He did not 'do that kind of thing'. Any flamboyance or boasting was totally foreign to his nature.

Nevertheless, within minutes – over-persuaded by someone, (I was out of sight and hearing by then) – he did speak those very words. All one can say is that he knew from the moment they left his lips that he had made a grave mistake, and had given a hostage to fortune that could break him and his political career.

I suppose it is possible to conclude that here was the genuine feeling of a man so saturated with his mission to conciliate that it had blinded him to all reality and to all rational thought. I do not believe that for one moment. He clung to the hope that peace might yet be saved, but from then on it was a hope and not a belief. All his life he had dealt with people who, although tough and sometimes ruthless in their bargains, had in the end made concession to reason. His miscalculation, which he shared with many others, was that he could not conceive that any man could positively prefer to get his way by war.

In fact, at the time of Munich, words had ceased to matter, for conciliation from that time forward was a lost cause.

Letter Nine

Before I come to sum up why we could not in the end escape the conclusion that there was no option left but to fight, I must deal with the question as to whether Chamberlain and the Government could have done anything else to deter Hitler from war.

To-day you are familiar with the military organization of Europe into the North Atlantic Treaty Organization and the Warsaw Pact, and you may well be asking how it was that Britain and France did not set about collecting an alliance which would have embraced more countries, and could have faced Germany with formidable opposition to her plans to expand.

There were several reasons. The first, as we have seen, was reliance on the League of Nations which was to be the substitute for alliances and military blocs; the second that Hitler had already talked Italy over to his side; and the third that the United States had opted for isolation, and had shown no sign whatever of interesting herself in Europe's squabbles.

During this difficult time there was one rather tentative approach to the British Government when President Roosevelt proposed that a conference of Ambassadors should be called to discuss the deteriorating situation in Europe. It was a vague proposal at a time when urgent action was required if Hitler was to be headed off from war, and Chamberlain judged that such a Conference would introduce an unacceptable delay, during which Hitler would continue to arm, and the chance of a negotiated settlement could easily go by default. In this judgement Chamberlain can fairly be said to have been wrong.

For the President of the United States to show a personal interest in Europe's problems was new, and could have led to the closer involvement of the one man in the world who really commanded the big battalions. It is true that America could not conceivably have taken any action which would have been effective in the time-scale set by Hitler's ambitions, and a Pearl Harbour was needed to enable the United States to break their neutrality. Nevertheless Chamberlain would have done well to have accepted the offer which was supported by Sir Ronald Lindsay, our very experienced Ambassador in Washington. Chamberlain, too, took the responsibility of sending rather a cool reply when Eden, his Foreign Secretary, was out of the country. The error was partly retrieved within months, but it should not have been made.

Then there was the question of Communist Russia. Could she be brought into some political and military Treaty arrangement which would face Hitler with the classic dilemma presented by a potential enemy on both flanks?

In 1938 negotiations were started, and they were spread over a good many months. There was one favourable factor which was that they were conducted in the beginning by Mr Litvinov, the Russian Foreign Minister, who was one of the few in the Communist hierarchy who had experience in foreign affairs. He was the man who had coined the phrase 'Peace is indivisible'.

But there is never anything straightforward in a negotiation with Russia, and political conditions were introduced into the talks which meant that, in return for agreement on common action with Britain and France, Russia would expect to be given a free hand to decide the future of the three hitherto independent countries – Latvia, Lithuania and Esthonia. There was no doubt in anyone's mind that the result would have been forcible incorporation of those Baltic States into the Soviet Union. It was impossible after Munich to stomach that.

However, even if a face-saving formula could have been found, the Russians at the very last moment insisted that a political agreement must be accompanied by precise military obligations, the first of which was that their armies should be guaranteed uninterrupted and unconditional passage through Poland.

That demand coincided with the dropping of Litvinov and the substitution of Molotov as chief Russian negotiator, and he was a master of inflexibility and of the technique of negative response.

The Russians, of course, knew very well that the Poles would not for one moment entertain their request, and so the negotiations were abortive. Who, with hindsight, can blame the Poles?

The question has been raised as to whether Litvinov had planned the breakdown from the start. Having negotiated with the Russians over many years I think it is more than likely that this was so. Litvinov, in all probability, formed a firm opinion early in the talks, on the comparative weakness of Britain and France, and decided that, seen from Russia's point of view, an alliance offered little attraction to his country. This interpretation of their action is reinforced by the speed with which, after the talks broke down, Russia signed a military pact with Germany. That could not have been achieved unless they had simultaneously been holding talks with both sides. The Russians were and are a cynical and unprincipled lot.

It was said, too, that if Sir William Strang, the able British Foreign Office official, had been replaced by a Minister the result might have been different. The Russian Communist mind, however, does not work in that way. If they had concluded that an alliance with Britain and France would have been advantageous for Russia they would have got it by hook or by crook. With the Russians no consideration but that of their own national interest is ever allowed to intrude. In the intervening years their technique in negotiation has been exactly the same. On that count Chamberlain can be exonerated from any blame.

So we came to the point where, if Hitler decided to use force yet again, war would have to be declared.

The British and French guarantee to Poland was not the ground on which any rational strategist would have chosen to fight, but there was no choice, for the Dictator had abused his power just as surely as Napoleon or the Kaiser, and a final halt had to be called.

It was Chamberlain who was fated to declare war, and he did not flinch from doing so. He became an efficient Chairman of the War Cabinet, but all his training had been in domestic politics, and his experience in years of peace. He did not know the language of war.

Churchill, on the other hand, in his early childhood days, had moved modern armies and fleets on the nursery floor, and had steeped himself in military history while he was still a young man. He had been blooded in war in South Africa, and had written extensively on military science and the conduct of campaigns.

He had, in the First War, been First Lord of the Admiralty, then Minister of Munitions, and subsequently Secretary of State for War and Air, and in each office had proved his dynamic qualities.

It happened, too, that events were so ordered by fate that they coincided with the peak of his intellectual powers. He recognized in himself the man of Britain's destiny, and so did the huge majority of his countrymen.

For once luck was on our side.

Letter Ten

I have assumed in these letters that you are not a pacifist – but you may well be asking yourself why it was that we found it necessary to fight in 1914, and again in 1939, when we knew only too well the hideous cost of war.

In the first case our instant reaction was partly outrage that the Kaiser should so rudely interrupt an era of unparalleled economic and social progress which held out the promise of even better things to come; but mainly moral indignation at the Germans' callous invasion of Belgium, a country which was in no sense a threat to them.

We had, of course, a self-interest in that with the European Continent subdued, Germany's ambition might have embraced the conquest of Britain, but in those days the English Channel was still thought to be so sure a guarantee against a successful invasion that we put first the fate of the Belgians who were so defenceless against the tyrant, and went to war on their behalf.

It is true that morality in those days was more

easily interpreted in black and white, and that internationally there were fewer grey areas than there are today, but the Kaiser had flouted the code of conduct of the Christian and democratic nations by his treatment of his weaker neighbours, so we did not need much persuading that we were on the side of right against wrong.

When our pioneers had founded the Empire they had the sword in one hand and the Bible in the other, and it was certainly true that it was the conviction that we were fighting on the side of the angels which carried us through those dark and dreadful years.

I am always careful before I bring morality into the political complexities of international affairs, but I thought then that we had right on our side, and I have not changed my mind.

By 1939 we knew the terrible price of war, and an opinion had begun to form (which had been entirely absent in 1914) that war was so evil a thing that surrender to a bully was almost better than the horror of a fight to the death.

The 1933 resolution of the Oxford undergraduates was not drafted or passed by cowards (many of them were soon to die as heroes) but because of a growing conviction that war was degrading to man who had a spark of divinity in him.

Chamberlain was only one of those in high places for whom war was so loathsome and sickening, that to preserve the peace he risked slipping over the edge of conciliation into appeasement. It is true that France carried the Treaty obligation to come to the help of Czecho-Slovakia, and Britain did not, but once again it was a moral line which had to be drawn. It was the conviction that Hitler was letting loose a flood of hatred so corrupting and evil in itself that convinced this country that we had to fight. Yet again an aggressor had torn up the Christian code of conduct, and we were sustained through the Battle of Britain, and all the military campaigns of those long years by the conviction that we were fighting on the side of right against devilish things.

That our instinct was correct was proved by the concentration camps in which the Nazis condemned the millions of European Jews to death. At the start of the war we did not know the scale and depth of such bestial behaviour and human degradation, but we sensed that evil was on the march, and morality counselled us to stand against it. We continued to do so even when we were left almost defenceless and alone.

What do you feel about the situation today? I have postponed asking that question as long as

I could for having been through two wars I pray that you will never have to answer it; but one has to admit that there are some ugly similarities between the situations then and now.

The doctrine held and practised by Communist Russia that a political aim may be furthered by force means that they are always engaged in brinkmanship, while the extent of their re-armament when others have stood still raises the fear that they may overstep the mark of prudence and face others with the dilemma of war or capitulation.

The evidence, too, that the Russians are careless of human rights, and are capable of ruthless oppression, introduces those questions of morality which so deeply stir the human emotions.

The last pose which we in Britain would wish to adopt is that of governess to the world, but there are certain standards and rules of conduct which have to be preserved between nations, if civilization is not to collapse and chaos to reign.

It would be all too easy to fall into the trap of self-righteousness. To such a posture the Russian Communist could properly object on the ground that terrible wars in the past have been waged in the name of the Christian religion, and that the record of the democracies is by no means clean. But in so far as we have put the past behind us, and have accepted the exhortation and standards of the Charter of the United Nations not to interfere in Russia's internal affairs, and in so far as we would certainly join in an International Treaty to safeguard and guarantee her against aggression from Germany, we are surely entitled to ask them so to act towards us. You will probably agree that proposition to be fair?

However, supposing that like Hitler, the Russian leadership proves to be impervious to reason, and events seem to be moving relentlessly towards another war, would you, like the unilateral disarmers and pacifists, throw in the towel? or would you, sustained by Christian and moral values which inspired and reinforced the British people in 1914 and 1939, take your stand?

I hasten to say that I do not expect you to answer that question off the cuff, for you now have a nuclear dimension added to war, and you will want time to consider whether the ultimate ethical and moral values apply to-day as they did in those earlier years. I will only add that I doubt if a society is worth preserving if it is not based on such values and a readiness to defend them.

Meanwhile, if you have the patience, I will bombard you with a further series of letters on the development of Communist Russia's international relations following her revolution. Then you will have all the facts on which to base a judgement.

Letter Eleven

To precede my promised bombardment on the policies of the Soviet Union here at long last is a piece of good news.

After the 1914 war the Communists of Russia and China were apparently happy bed-fellows, and they represented themselves as a 'bloc' which was hostile to the Western world. Then they split, and in so far as they have a relationship now it is one in which the Chinese hold the Russians at arms' length.

An interpretation of the ideological difference between them is difficult for the Western mind to make. Mr Chou-en-Lai told me that the Russians translated the Communist doctrine as authorizing subversion even against countries with whom they had diplomatic relations, and as entitling them if necessary to use force to achieve their purpose. He went on to say that China repudiated such a proposition. However that may be there were other and more tangible reasons for their quarrel and separation.

After the Long March, the Russians, with apparent good will, had given to the Chinese a lot of technical help in their programme of industrialization, and in particular were building for them a large complex for the production of steel. Without warning their technicians were ordered off the plant by the Russian Government, leaving behind them a skeleton of bricks and steel. The Chinese have not forgotten what they still label an act of treachery and industrial sabotage which could have been fatal to their prospects.

Then there was the fact of Russia's behaviour on the frontier of three thousand miles. When, as sometimes happened in the wild and open spaces, nomads from China followed their flocks into Russian territory, the reaction of the Kremlin was always harsh and hostile, and the Russian forces on the frontier were continuously increased far beyond the needs of local policing.

When I was in Peking in 1971 the Chinese leadership had persuaded themselves that there was a real danger that the Russians would use force to destroy their nuclear installations, and set back their industrial progress yet again. Every city was honey-combed with air-raid shelters. It seemed to me then that the unity of the Communist bloc was irrevocably smashed.

The main anxiety of Chinese ministers at that time was that Western Europe would fail to understand the reality of the Russian threat to our Continent. They emphasized from their experience of Russia's thinking that the democracies of Europe were in the Soviet's eyes the main obstacle to the communization of the world, and they judged that if the NATO alliance showed any weakness that the Russians would attack. The Chinese considered that the crunch would come in the early eighties.

Later they were to have their opinion of Russia's duplicity confirmed when the North Vietnamese were reinforced with Soviet weaponry to such a point that they posed a serious military threat to mainland China, and caused the Chinese defence forces to be mobilized.

All these experiences have induced China not only to break with the Soviet Union, but to turn to the West for assistance with her industrial development. It is a sensational turnover in international politics and in the balance of power.

I never saw the Long March through rose-coloured spectacles; on the contrary when Mao-tse-Tung was in command I placed him in the same class as Stalin for ruthlessness and abuse of power.

To-day the Chinese are still Communists. In modern China there is direction of labour, and little freedom for the individual as in the West we would understand it. But they are Communists with a difference. They have understood (because they have had a taste of it) the Kremlin's ambitions in terms of territorial power, and they do not wish to see Russia dominate the world.

In an unofficial moment I asked Mr Chou-en-Lai about China's intentions towards Hong Kong. He answered obliquely with a question as to whether I remembered India's actions in relation to the small Portuguese enclave of Goa? I said that I did, and that in my view Prime Minister Nehru had been guilty of a gross abuse of power. Chou-en-Lai said: 'Well, you may be sure that nothing like Goa will ever take place over Hong Kong.'

In view of its history of dominance by warlords who made their own laws and ruled by arms, prophecy about China's future is hazardous. But, if alongside their new national unity they accept the need for restraint in the use of power, that can make all the difference to the prospect of peace for the world.

There was one marked difference in negotiations with Chinese and Russians. One could say to a Chinese politician that their Communism needed a good deal more explanation and justification than it had been given up to now, and he would laugh and argue, and both parties would enjoy a civilized exchange of views. Say the same to a Russian and the reply would be: 'Such a subject is not appropriate for discussion.' I know because I tried many times and was always treated to the same formula in reply.

I would sum up China's relations with the Soviet Union as one of cool co-existence with a wary eye.

Letter Twelve

You may have guessed that I mean to miss out the years, 1939–45.

When the war started I remember that we knew little about the impact of air-power, but our imagination worked overtime, and we anticipated that most of Britain would be obliterated by bombs. Our cities did suffer terrible punishment, but the spirit of the people was not broken, and we endured and survived.

Towards the end Hitler's 'doodle-bugs' (the early land-to-land missiles) were unnerving, and I remember your grandmother reacting to the unearthly strangeness of them by putting up her umbrella as protection as one flew over our heads when we were walking in St James's Park! You heard them coming with a steady engine-beat, but when they cut out someone was for it somewhere.

But by then the land battle on the continent was near its end, and the Germans resigned to defeat.

When victory came we had learned some lessons from the earlier peace-making. There was no disposition to allow the German army to claim for a second time that it had not really been beaten. It was pursued and destroyed.

On the other hand no one clamoured for reparations which would squeeze Germany so hard as to make the 'pips squeak'. Quite the contrary, for Sir Anthony Eden and the other allied Ministers recognized that the best surety for peace lay in bringing Germany into the Western alliance, and by so doing substitute trust for fear, and partnership for lack of security.

The Germans, in their search for economic recovery, had a natural advantage in the discipline which has always been part of their make-up, but they also had a bit of luck in having Herr Erhard in charge of the rebuilding of their finances. He saw immediately that there was no short cut to prosperity, and that there was no substitute for work, and he persuaded the German people and the Trade Unions to knuckle down to a long hard slog of recovery.

His own accomplishments and personality won for him recognition abroad, and brought about that confidence in Germany's performance which was essential if she was to prosper.

The Germans also chose Adenauer as Chancellor. He was keenly aware that the image of Germany in the eyes of Europe and the world had to be completely changed, and that he must show the people the new road.

He had the advantage that he had no taint of Nazism, and he knew within himself that for the future the physical security of Germany must derive not from her own military might, but from alliance with those European neighbours who had lately been Germany's enemies.

He had a dominating presence. He was getting on in years when I knew him, and had an arresting and almost alarming appearance, for his head and face looked for all the world like a pickled walnut – colour, wrinkles, texture and all!

It was said that he reinforced his natural vitality with some kind of treatment with an extract from the gland of a monkey. I suspect that this idea derived from his wizened looks, but if this was so he was the best of advertisements for it, for well into his eighties he had a mind which was as clear as a bell, and an authority which was unchallenged.

I cannot think of any other German who could have sold to the people the idea of rapprochement with France as the basis for the economic and political unity of Europe. The German nation is deeply in his debt.

When the minds of Conrad Adenauer and General de Gaulle met and clicked the Gods really declared themselves on Europe's side; for unless these two men had agreed to act over the heads of their electors the foundations simply would not have been there on which to build a united Europe.

De Gaulle only came into my life after the war, and therefore when his character had become less angular and abrasive than it was when he first crossed to England as the representative of the Free French.

Then such different men as Chamberlain, Eden and Churchill found the difficulty of working with him to be almost intolerable but something must be allowed for a proud man deeply wounded by the humiliation of his country's surrender to the enemy.

Like Adenauer he had a clear conception of the future rôle of France. He knew that the only way by which the French could regain their self-respect would be if they pulled themselves out of the slough of despond unbeholden to anyone else. That was why France declined to become a member of the NATO alliance, although giving it independent support; that is why de Gaulle refused to accept the American Polaris missile system. He identified himself with France, and saw to it that patriotism was the inspiration of every act of policy. No other Frenchman could have induced the French people to evacuate Algeria in the name of husbanding and consolidating the strength of metropolitan France.

In his later years he became reckless. The cry of 'vive le Québec libre' on his visit to Canada was pure and irresponsible mischief.

I remember that on one of his visits to Mr Macmillan he proposed that we, the British, should take some action in relation to the Soviet Union which he was not prepared to recommend to his own Government, but which he thought he might be able to foist on us. After listening politely, I said, 'But, General, the proposition is preposterous. If we succeed you have arranged for the French to take all the credit, and if we fail you will say "I told you so". You are trying to get the best of both worlds.' To which his reply was, 'Yes, my boy, and what is wrong with that?'!

Adenauer and de Gaulle were just two more examples of how in politics people matter. For it was essentially these two men who brought about the rebirth of their countries.

There was one other mistake which we avoided with the lesson of 1918 learned. We recognized that if there was to be a successor to the League of Nations that its membership must be universal. In the event the earlier absentees – America and Russia – signed the new Charter of the United Nations, while Germany was soon admitted to membership. Prudently on this occasion Britain was not swept by euphoria. We had been through too much to put our faith in anything but fact, and in this case the proof of the pudding had to be in the eating.

Russia's continuing emphasis on the need for a veto was scarcely encouraging, nevertheless here was another chance for the world to find a better way to settle disputes than by war. It turned out to be a fleeting opportunity as Russia increasingly cold-shouldered co-operation to the point of conducting a cold war. They posed, and they still pose, the question as to whether like Hitler they prefer to get their way by force. We just do not know the answer to that. The only measures by which we can make a judgement are first their actions over the years, and secondly, by constantly trying to interpret the very few hints and noises which come out of the Kremlin.

It is extraordinarily difficult to read the Russian mind, but in the next letter or two I must have a shot at it.

Letter Thirteen

Although Csar Nicholas II was a man who desired to do well by his people and had a fund of human understanding, he was in fact carefully isolated from the public, and sat on a shaky throne.

The picture of the poverty and misery of the Russian peasants had spread abroad and had generated some sympathy in liberal circles outside for the aims of Lenin's popular revolution.

It was true that to corrupt young soldiers at the front was seditious and sabotaged the allied military operations against the German aggressor; true, too, that the cold-blooded slaughter of the Imperial family could not be condoned; nevertheless the Communists proclaimed the championship of the weak and the poor, and pledged themselves to replace autocracy by the people's will.

Europe was war-weary, and gave the Russian revolutionaries the benefit of the doubt. After all, with the defeat of the Germans in 1918, and the toll of the Russian dead, there was no need to include Russia in the scales of power.

The first clue to the true nature of the Communist régime came with the bloody purge of 'deviationists' in the late thirties when there were wholesale murders and deportations to Siberia. Even then the external reaction was muted. The Russian people had chosen Communism, and if that was what they liked let them have it so long as it did not bother anyone else.

That proviso, however, contained the snag, for after war had consolidated Stalin in power, he interpreted Marxist doctrine as justifying Russia in using force to achieve a political aim wherever her ambition might lead.

The first hint which came to me that Stalin would require a 'cordon-sanitaire' in Eastern Europe as a price for Russia's alliance in war, came from information I received from the Tehran Conference of 1943. There was little that Churchill and Roosevelt could do to counter the blackmail as Russia had to be held in the war if the defeat of Germany was to be ensured; but it was an ominous sign that the fate of a country such as Poland did not arouse in Stalin even a twinge of conscience.

If, in the eyes of the Kremlin, the Russian interest required that the independence of the countries of Eastern Europe should be extinguished, that would be done.

Later at the Yalta Conference, just before the war ended, the Americans and the British tried to introduce the concept of free and democratic elections for the Poles, to which Stalin paid lip-service, but which he had no intention of conceding on the day. It was a callous exhibition of unrestrained power.

Nor after thirty-five years have the Russians modified their policy, for, as you have seen, they have lately added Afghanistan to the buffer states. They are thus capable of setting a political aim and of pursuing and sustaining it over a long period of time.

It was in relation to Stalin's gross appetite that Churchill said:

'A bear in the forest is a proper matter for
    speculation;
A bear in the zoo is a proper matter for
    public curiosity;
A bear in your wife's bed is a matter of the
    gravest concern.'

Even after this exhibition of blatant militarism Russia would have been welcomed into the comity of nations. Her representative was in fact present and actively engaged in the drafting of the Charter of the new United Nations. Not only that, but Russia signed the Charter which included the pledge not to interfere in the internal affairs of her neighbours. It was true that she had insisted on the right of the permanent members of the Security Council to a veto, but her friends and allies had invited her co-operation in solving the world's problems, and here was the opportunity to show it.

The first firm sign that came to me that she intended to cold-shoulder the democracies was not however in the military context, but was concerned with Marshall Aid. That imaginative and generous scheme, sponsored by the United States, was designed to assist the countries of Europe, including the Soviet Union, to repair the economic damage inflicted in the war.

Russia, of course, could properly have refused to accept such help on the grounds that for reasons of internal morale she would prefer to pull herself up by her own bootstraps. In fact she turned down the proposal with scant courtesy and near contempt, with the words that agreement would involve an 'unacceptable infringement of Russia's sovereignty'.

Since then Russia's leaders have been totally consistent, and have refused to play any part in the international agencies for aid and development. Once again they showed themselves capable of laying down a policy and sticking to it over decades however much world conditions might change.

So the new Communist leaders had deliberately turned their backs on two opportunities for partnership with the democracies. The first by their vetoes in the Security Council on peacemaking; the second by declining to join in a common effort to restore economic advance.

Once again they had served notice that they preferred tepid co-existence to co-operation. On the evidence they still do so to-day.

With the benefit of hindsight it was clearly naïve to assume that peace was the natural order for men who were part of the animal creation, but why was it that the Russians who had suffered so acutely in war, and the Communists who had preached the virtues of the universal socialist society and the brotherhood of man, spurned so ostentatiously the hand of friendship? For if ever there was a chance to break down social barriers, to dilute the economic doctrine of capitalism and to break away from the confrontation of alliances and blocs it was then.

The lesson has been taught time and time again that it is unwise to try and separate a people from their history, and Russians have traditionally been abnormally secretive and suspicious of foreigners. The diaries of travellers in the 18th and 19th centuries are reflected exactly in the frustrations inflicted by Communist officials today.

The conclusion which seems to be inescapable is that Russians prefer to act alone and to be feared rather than loved. That could be acceptable to the rest were it not for the fact that the Russian Communist feels entitled to disrupt his neighbour's life on the theory that chaos anywhere contributes to Russia's security. Being beholden to none is one thing, being responsible to none another.

The reason why Communist Russia is a source of running anxiety to those countries with stable institutions is clearly illustrated by placing two statements by their leaders alongside each other.

The first is that of Mr Brezhnev that the future is one of perpetual struggle, ending with the words 'The purpose of Russian Communism is ultimate victory over every other way of life'. The second, the words of a late Secretary-General of the Communist Party: 'We do not desire to use force, but we cannot allow the lack of it to stand in the way of our political aims'. There, in a nutshell, is the reason why fear has stalked abroad for thirty years, and why it still walks today.

Of course these might be the boastings of braggarts, so their words must be measured against the facts. Do they mean what they say? Czecho-Slovakia and Afghanistan argue that they do. So, too, do their actions in Asia and Africa.

It is, however, necessary to probe even deeper into their motives, for upon reaching the correct answer hangs the nature of the political and military strategy of the free and democratic world.

The Communist book of doctrine caters for the direct use of force, as in the cases of Czecho-Slovakia and Afghanistan or in the sponsorship of force by others as in Vietnam, Angola, Ethiopia and South America, but it also allows and seems to prefer that where possible the political goal shall be fixed and reached by stealth. The advance therefore towards the target may be punctuated by tactical retreat designed to lull the intended victim into a false sense of security, until the coup de grâce is given.

I witnessed these techniques carried out to perfection by Mr Gromyko in relation to the future fate of South Vietnam and Cambodia.

The object of the peace-making exercise in Asia in which Britain and France, America and China were engaged was to achieve the neutrality of Laos, Cambodia and North and South Viet-

nam, and thus avoid the clash of great powers.
The two means by which this could be done
were first by limiting the armaments authorized
to those needed for the internal policing of those
states, and secondly by stopping the importation
of arms from abroad. In other words 'non-intervention' put into practice.

The machinery to supervise the process was
available, and India, a leading non-aligned
country, was persuaded to act as Chairman of
an International Commission. The Russians
would not agree to a general oversight by the
United Nations, nevertheless the scene was set
in the area for a successful exercise in disarmament and for co-operation for peace, in which
the local representatives of political factions had
also concurred.

After tough negotiations the Soviet Union
signed a Treaty which agreed the conditions and
established the machinery, and charged the
Foreign Ministers of Russia and Britain with the
general supervision of progress.

From the moment of signature in 1954 the
Russians made the work of the Commission
impossible by encouraging the North Vietnamese to intransigence, and continuing to supply
them with arms on a large scale.

By 1960 there was confusion amounting to

chaos, and I invited Mr Gromyko to re-assemble
the Conference. Eventually he agreed, and a long
meeting followed which again set up a reinforced
International Commission with explicit terms of
procedure and a plan of action.

Immediately the same obstruction began with
North Vietnam receiving and obeying Russia's
instructions, and the work of the Commission
was paralysed.

There had been two tactical retreats followed
by militancy. There was to be a repeat performance in 1971 when a Third Treaty was agreed,
and signed, only for the same farce to be repeated.

This was a classic example of the conduct of
Russia's foreign policy; the political target fixed –
the build-up of force – the tactical withdrawal to
placate hostile opinion, and then the final strike
when overwhelming strength was used.

Dr Kissinger has written a most detailed and
authentic account of this terrible Vietnam story.
The responsibility for the tragedy of the Boatpeople must be laid directly at Russia's door.

The Soviet Union nearly over-stepped the line
set by their doctrine of alternate advance–retreat–
advance, for they continued to re-arm the North
Vietnamese to a point where they posed an
active threat to mainland China. The Chinese, a
Communist society educated in the same school

as the leaders of the Kremlin, were faced with the dilemma either to endure the provocation of the build-up of strength on their borders, or themselves to use force in reply to that mobilized by North Vietnam. With all its risks – for they were inadequately armed – they decided to serve notice that at the next provocation their target would be Hanoi. That is as clear a case as can be found of the deliberate aggravation of a local situation so as to create the maximum of chaos. It is a classic case of the dilemma with which Communism confronts the democracies.

There would seem to be several lessons to be learned from this. The first that weakness is always a temptation to a totalitarian régime. The second that Communist Russia works by the book. In the case of Vietnam she used the tactical retreat, while over fifteen years her eye was firmly on the political goal. The third, as is proved by North Vietnam's aggression against China, that the Russian leaders are ready to indulge in brinkmanship if the prize would decisively turn the balance of power in their favour.

A British Ambassador once wrote in a dispatch: 'It is impossible to exaggerate the danger of the situation here, but I will do my best'. I always give myself that caution when I write about the Russians.

The Communist revolution is now more than sixty years old, and it is always possible that the rules of the Red Book may be modified; but a sober analysis of events over all those years reveals that their purpose is still to undermine stability because any weakening of other régimes and settled ways of life is calculated to redound to their advantage.

Democracies, if they are true to their nature, can never abandon conciliation, but common prudence insists that they should sup with Russian Communism with a long spoon.

I hope I have been able to illustrate to you the horrible choice which constantly faces the democracies. Our instincts are all for the quiet life, so that we may concentrate the benefits of scientific development on the betterment of men and women. Massive sums spent annually on re-armament clearly frustrate this purpose, but what alternative have we if the Russians insist on forcing the pace in the interest of a Communist take-over?

We have allowed our defences to fall behind in the hope that example might influence the Kremlin, but so far it has pocketed the concessions and gone on its military way.

It is dreadfully like Hitler isn't it?

Letter Fourteen

The really extraordinary thing about the Russian Communist leaders is that they have been able to stamp their will upon their people for so long.

The movement started, as we have seen, with the inspiration and momentum of a high ideal. In the new order each was to put his share into the economic pool, and all were to work for the State. All exploitation was to be abolished, and social justice would arrive with the formula 'from each according to his ability – to each according to his need'.

However, the economic theory never worked. Time after time the peasants and the citizens of the towns were exhorted to achieve new targets of production, but they failed to reach them, and in place of expanding their prospects all had to tighten their belts.

Forced labour was employed; scapegoats were found and statistics were manipulated; but nothing could conceal the fact that by comparison with any other country in Europe life in Russia was indescribably unproductive and drab.

Nor, following Stalin's corruption of the Socialist ideal, was there physical security for the individual, for the secret police were instructed to weed out the deviators from the strict Party doctrine, and to dispose of them by exile to Siberia or by death. In a block of flats, for example, one family would silently disappear from time to time, so that the rest would learn that conformity was wise.

The result was that, except for the few who were favoured in politics or the armed services or in sport or in the Ballet, the majority lived in suspicion and fear. This was made clear immediately to the visitor from abroad by the hang-dog way the people in Moscow went about their business in the streets. It was a terrifying example of how the human spirit can be subdued.

In 1962 the extent of the ignorance about people and events outside the Soviet Union was profound. As we left Moscow Airport after signing the Test Ban Treaty, Mrs Gromyko, who was a nice and friendly woman, brought a present for your grandmother. It was a string bag full of tinned tomatoes and carrots, given half apologetically, because she had heard how hard-up for food we were in Britain. She was the wife of the Foreign Minister, and we were basking in the period when 'we never had it so good'!

I was able to measure a degree of advance in Russia's economic and social advance over a period of ten years. In 1962 we were guests at a gala performance of the Bolshoi Ballet with an invited audience. All the men were dressed in boiler suits or working clothes, and all the women in shapeless black or dark grey. The contrast with the stage was as a slum to fairyland. In 1973, with a similar audience, the men were dressed in suits which, if uniformly square-cut, were tidy, while the women were in varying shades of grey or dark blue. Such was the pace of concession to the consumer society.

Doubtless there has been further progress in the last ten years, but the Russians are still, by contrast with Europeans, backward, and very insecure in themselves, particularly when they are in contact with foreigners.

I once asked Mr Gromyko to send a lot of Russian young to meet a comparable number of British boys and girls at work and play. His reply was 'I would not like to expose our young people to the decadence of your modern youth'. I defended you with spirit (I hope I was right?), but of course his failure to respond was due to the fact that he did not dare to allow young Communists to get a taste for the liberties which are a commonplace in our democratic society.

They use ignorance as a shield against freedom. This suspicion and obsession with security made all of their politicians exceedingly dull. The only exception from that generalization was Kruschev. He came from a peasant stock in the Ukraine, and had a kind of crude, earthy and bawdy humour, which he exploited usually at someone else's expense. If any of that lot had a streak of liberalism with the smallest of 'l's' I suppose it was he, but I could not like him.

In politics one has to mix with all sorts, and some of them ruffians, but it is not possible to be at ease with one who has liquidated thousands so as to hoist himself into political power.

Nor, like most bullies, did Kruschev like it when he was given a taste of his own medicine.

In those days it was fashionable for our Parliamentary Socialist Party to entertain the 'comrades' when they came to London, and when at one of these luncheons George Brown interjected a crude expletive into one of Kruschev's more outrageous extravagances of speech, he was not amused.

Likewise, when Harold Macmillan, with more finesse, asked for a translation of some farmyard abuse which was being slung at Britain in the United Nations Assembly, Kruschev scowled at the amused reaction of the audience.

I expect you will have heard of the incident, also in New York, when he took off his shoe and beat on the rostrum in the Assembly to underline his contempt for the Americans. The result, of course, was ridiculous, but it was typical of the sort of ill-tempered impetuosity which eventually cost him his office.

To try and plant nuclear missiles in Cuba in order to teach the Americans a lesson in Russian power, was totally farcical, for unless he was prepared to face all-out war, which he was not, the Russian fleet was bound to retreat in disorder. His colleagues had not felt strong enough to curb his exuberance, but they had digested the rule in the Red Book which instructs that superior force is not to be challenged head-on. They have kept to it ever since.

After Kruschev I concluded that dullness is a positive virtue!

Brezhnev was entirely different. A child of the new industrial revolution and of the city; a dedicated, dour and careful servant of the Communist State. He pursued the orthodox policy laid down by the revolution; he strengthened the buffer protection on Russia's borders; he intervened on the side of revolutionary movements overseas, for it is the doctrine that political confusion anywhere pays a dividend; above all he believed that the Soviet Union, having won a marginal advantage in arms by courtesy (as he would have put it) of gullible potential enemies, must hold on to that prize.

The Russian leader for whom over the years I began to have a certain admiration – even affection – was (and is) Mr Gromyko. But even with him one's feelings had to be modified and controlled by the knowledge that he would put the Soviet Union's signature to a Treaty, and then cheat without batting an eyelid. To allow him to think that one had been hood-winked was fatal, as he would pocket the point at issue as acquiescence; so I always had to let him know that I knew exactly what he and his colleagues were up to. You can imagine how laborious such constant vigilance was and is, for the techniques of Russian diplomacy have not changed.

Apart from Gromyko, Mr Dobrynin, their Ambassador in Washington, was fully equipped to hold his own in world diplomacy, but generally they were a dour lot.

Reluctantly, but certainly, I came to one positive conclusion, that the Russian leaders would always take advantage of weakness, but – and here is a crumb of comfort – that they would not challenge equal or superior strength.

In another letter I will look at what that implies

for the Western alliance on the ground in strategy and tactics. Above everything it means that the democracies must keep their nerve. More than ever is that so in this age of nuclear power.

Letter Fifteen

Before we look at the moral problems involved in using nuclear weapons as a deterrent to war, I must tell you that I have experienced two occasions after the last war when Western nerves were taut.

The first was when the Russians tried to change the quadripartite nature of the government of Berlin by blocking all access by road and rail. Unless the land routes into the city were to be forced, the only approach which was open was along an air corridor crossing East German territory.

Unless the British and the Americans and the French were to knuckle under there was no alternative but to organize a massive air-lift to keep the inhabitants alive. This was done, and the onus was put squarely on the Russians either to enforce a total blockade by shooting our planes down, which would have been an act of war, or to abandon their ill-considered scheme.

After three weeks it was the Russians' nerve which cracked.

There was never a threat of nuclear war as the Americans held such an over-whelming advantage in weaponry, but a 'conventional' fight could have begun of which it would have been difficult to see the end.

Some years later Russian bombers began to drop metal chaff in the flight-path of our aeroplanes which rendered the instruments on which the pilots relied for landing and take-off unstable. Luckily Dean Rusk and I were in Geneva with Mr Gromyko. We made forcible representations to him that his government's action was totally irresponsible, and that if there was an accident we could not answer for the consequences. After a lot of bluster and some tense moments while he consulted his government, he returned and said that we had invented the accusation, and that it was totally false. He added, with a poker face, that as chaff had never been dropped we could be assured that it could not happen in the future. We drank his health, and went to bed.

But those incidents were nothing compared to the critical moment when Mr Kruschev tried to install nuclear missiles in Cuba, and take the threat to the very door-step of the United States.

The sequence of events was something like this. The Americans had established a lead over Russia in the production of inter-continental ballistic missiles of around five to one, and Mr Kruschev, looking round for some short cut to countering American superiority, thought up the idea of planting Russia's offensive missiles in Cuba.

The proposition was not as militarily crazy as it looked, for if America had not re-acted, and sixty missiles had been put in place, Russia's nuclear strike capacity would have been doubled. Kruschev was therefore egged on in the gamble by his military advisers.

Castro, the Cuban leader, had already been outraged and frightened by an attempted landing by some American-raised forces in the Bay of Pigs, and it was in his interest to entangle Russia as deeply as possible in the defence of his island against American occupation. He too therefore encouraged the Kruschev adventure.

Soon after Kennedy became President he had met Kruschev in Vienna. The latter was well-versed and fully briefed on the international situation, and Kennedy showed that he was at a disadvantage. Kruschev's natural cockiness and egotism was reinforced, and he came away from the meeting convinced that he could make rings round this raw young man, and could twist America's tail with impunity. It was a personal error of judgement which before very long was to cost Kruschev his office. However for some days during the Cuban adventure the world seemed to hold its breath.

Neither Britain nor France was consulted, but we were informed as events unfolded, and because President Kennedy had a high opinion of Mr Macmillan's wisdom, experience and judgement the line to Washington was really hot.

Incidentally it was lucky Mr Kruschev was not listening-in for neither of these great men was good at the mechanics of the 'hot line', and the private secretaries had to be constantly enlisted to give technical aid.

But broadly the questions were two:

How should America react? and if the decision was to intercept the Soviet Fleet, how far towards Cuba should it be allowed to sail?

As early as August Kennedy had warned the Russians that the United States would have to act if ground-to-ground missiles were placed in Cuba. We in Britain could not see how he could do otherwise.

Yet in September the Tass agency in the Soviet Union was still saying that missiles could be landed on the island without retaliation, and in the last week of October the fleet actually sailed with its deadly cargo.

The Russian fleet consisted of twenty-five

ships, including submarines, and it seemed that Kruschev was too deeply committed to withdraw. All American forces, including the nuclear, were therefore put on full alert. That was high drama.

There were plenty of alarms and excursions. An American U2 reconnaissance plane was shot down over Cuba, and another was identified over Russian territory. Did this presage a preemptive nuclear strike by the United States with long-range intercontinental missiles?

Kennedy's tactics were to convey to the Russians the sternest of warnings, and simultaneously to give Kruschev the maximum time in which to order a retreat. In this he was ably supported by his brother Bobby, the Attorney-General. This reaction coincided with the views expressed by Macmillan.

The President then devised the lowest key response consistent with security. He announced that a 'quarantine' of Cuba would be imposed in relation to nuclear weapons. Even the word 'blockade' was rejected as being likely to recall memories of the American–Spanish–Cuban war of 1898.

At some time in that fateful week Kruschev's nerve had faltered, and he reverted to the possibility of a bargain which he had floated some days earlier. It was to the effect that, in return for an American promise not to invade Cuba, Russia would remove the offending missiles from the island.

Bobby Kennedy immediately saw the significance and the possibilities in the formula, provided that the withdrawal was supervised by the United Nations.

Within 24 hours Russia's acceptance came, and the crisis was past.

The Russian leader had carried brinkmanship to the end and lost. Never since then have the Soviet leaders looked like issuing a direct military challenge to the United States.

I have written at some length on this incident because it illustrates so clearly the dangers of playing around with nuclear weapons. The lesson which the Russians learned must be taken in by all of us.

I trust you will never have to go through such an experience, for there were times when I understood what is meant by one's hair standing on end!

PS I ought really to have added this to my letter on the Cuban crisis, but I must have been exhausted emotionally by my recollections, and I forgot to make a point which holds the secret to any normalization of relations with the Soviet Union.

The rule is always to maintain an even-tempered approach, and always to explain in words of one syllable the purpose of any action taken. Once they know exactly where they stand with a Western country they will adapt their diplomacy to that situation. Blow hot and then cold and they will find the temptation to exploit differences to be irresistible.

The same is true of the NATO alliance, and of the Council of Europe. Far the most successful exercise which we conducted in the context of East–West relations stemmed from the trouble taken to co-ordinate an allied point of view on the approaches to the Helsinki Conference.

The Russians could find no reason for not signing on the dotted line, and committing themselves publicly to embarking on the road to détente. They broke their pledged word when they invaded Afghanistan, but if you want a model for negotiation with Communist Russia look up the terms of the Helsinki Final Act.

If co-operation is ever to take the place of cold co-existence Helsinki points the way.

Letter Sixteen

It is always easier to pose a dilemma than to find the answer to it, but in this final batch of letters I must try to answer the question what, if Russia maintains the challenging posture, do the democracies do? and then to tempt fortune by trying to foresee the circumstances in which a change for the better might occur.

I remember that in an earlier letter I wrote that when in 1939 the air-raid warnings screeched out their message, we anticipated that London at least would be blown to bits, and although we trooped into the shelters in an orderly and humorously British way our hearts were in our mouths.

We had had no experience of air attack, and imagination ran riot, although it never could have conceived of anything as awful as the later experience of Hiroshima and Nagasaki.

Now we know, and although the techniques of interception of aircraft and missiles have improved enormously, some will penetrate the barrier and every sense revolts against such wanton destruction of life and property.

So fearful indeed is the prospect that some argue that the pursuit of nuclear knowledge should be halted, and that nuclear power, in spite of its inestimable benefit for civilian use, should be banned. Everyone must concede the horror of a nuclear explosion, but I do not find the pacifists' position valid or practical. One might as well argue that the healing power of drugs should be denied to the sick because they are capable of wholesale corruption of the young.

There are very few ingredients of God's creation so evil as to justify the suppression of knowledge, and nuclear power has certainly come to stay.

Man, however, has the gift of choice. In the last war he chose to light and heat his house with gas, but to eschew the use of the poisonous varieties to maim and suffocate his enemies. So it can be with nuclear energy and chemicals, for man can be selective in the purposes for which he uses, and the limits which he places on the gifts of God. If he claims to be civilized that is a responsibility which he cannot shirk. For misuse he must substitute control.

The easiest of the options is for those who confront each other to open their installations and arsenals to inspection. So far it is the Russians who have blocked all such proposals. More of that later, but, frustrated by deadlock in working out a programme for mutual and balanced disarmament which can be verified and controlled, there are an increasing number of sincere and well-meaning people who urge that the only hope which remains is that Britain should unilaterally renounce her nuclear arm even though its sole purpose is to deter aggression.

A matter which contains the elements of life and death on such a scale clearly has a moral content on which each should consult his own conscience. My present contribution must be that during many years of face-to-face negotiation with Russian leaders I never found a shred of evidence to support the view that they could be disarmed by example.

On the contrary there is reason to think that talk of unilateral disarmament encourages them to believe that, if they keep up the pressures on the democracies, they will gain their point without any quid pro quo. We, for example, renounced germ warfare only to see the Russians increase their stocks and their preparations.

From my experience, should we make the nuclear gesture, the sole result would be that the Russians would pocket the bonus and continue exactly as before, with their forces backed by nuclear power.

If we are to concede our nuclear weapons it must be part of a disarmament deal. Here I must put the ball squarely into the unilateralists' court.

What is wrong, morally or practically, with 'mutual and balanced' disarmament? Is it not transparently fair?

It is true that over many years the formula has not produced results, but the fact that one side has stalled the negotiations surely does not render the concept invalid?

Mutuality could not, of course, be worked out with such precision as to balance each gun and each tank, but it could provide for a reduction of forces and arms by each side so that the temptation to aggression would lose its attraction. Control and reduction of conventional weapons is important, for a war is very unlikely to begin by a nuclear power using a first strike; far more likely that it could start from a local confrontation getting out of hand.

The reality of the matter is that at best it will take some years to talk the Soviet leaders into accepting arms control at much reduced levels, so what do the democracies and the NATO alliance do in the meanwhile?

If you have accepted my contention that unilateral disarmament would be a futile gesture, that means that we still have to rely on a balance of power.

If that is our conclusion then the equation must be real in the sense that there must be enough allied forces on land and sea and in the air to make the risk of aggression too high until the required disarmament is achieved. It will be expensive, and a test of our will, but it will be cheaper than war.

At present there is a somewhat esoteric argument proceeding as to whether the British nuclear deterrent should be Polaris with a somewhat extended life, or the new Trident. I go for the latter because the Americans have scrapped Polaris, and if we delay the opportunity to take Trident, it may be difficult or impossible in the future to get into the American production lines.

It is also argued that, apart from the American and Russian deterrents, every nuclear force is superfluous. The short answer to that is 'tell it to the French'! Logically a case can be made that, if the intention is never to use the weapon, then it is wrong to pose the threat. But logic doesn't always apply when, as in this case, the threat is probably enough to deter.

It is always prudent too to try and put oneself into the potential enemy's mind. Which would the Russians prefer, a Britain contributing to the

Western balance of power? or a Britain unilaterally disarmed? You will not need me to spell
out the answer. If they wish us to discard our
nuclear arm let them come to the table and strike
a disarmament bargain.

I started this letter by saying I must tackle the
question what we as a nation should do, but first
I must be clear what we should not do, and that
is unilaterally to disarm.

I will add one further comment. It is often said
that the nuclear weapon is immoral when its sole
purpose is to deter war. I do not believe that it is
profitable to label this weapon or that weapon.
What is immoral is to use brinkmanship and
force in a nuclear age. What is immoral is
aggression and war.

I start from the premise that all wars of aggression, with whatever arms may be used, are immoral, and that there are in the world evil men
who plan to impose their will upon others by
force.

Czecho-Slovakia and Afghanistan – to say
nothing of Poland and the Berlin wall – witness
to the truth of that.

Against such harsh facts of history I can find
nothing in the Christian teaching which denies
to me or to my companions in democracy, the
right to defend life and the basic values which

make it worth living, against those who aim to destroy them.

Still less can I convince myself that it is un-christian to seek to deter a potential aggressor by making the risk of war too high.

From there I proceed to analyse the doctrine (or religion) of the Russian Communist régime.

The doctrine proclaims the right to use force in support of a political aim, and the witnesses named above testify that the theory is put into practice.

But it also instructs that military force shall not be deployed if it is likely to meet superior or equal strength.

In such a situation the order of the day is to beat a tactical retreat against a future occasion when the opponent drops his guard. That is a powerful argument in favour of deterrence.

Provided therefore that the democracies are prepared to negotiate with the Russians on multi-lateral disarmament I conclude that in the meanwhile a policy of equality of strength not only passes the test of morality, but is most likely to keep the peace.

Letter Seventeen

By ringing the changes on subversion and force, and in particular by maintaining large armies in Eastern Europe the Russians place a considerable strain on the economics of the democracies.

That, of course, is done by design as one of the pressures which are calculated to break the capitalist system. This objective Russia has equally failed to achieve, but the burden of armaments has compelled the West to set priorities.

For example the security of Western Europe and the Atlantic Ocean has had to be given preference over the South Atlantic and the Indian Ocean.

With the end of colonial rule the area of British and European responsibility for law and order sharply contracted.

When for instance the British administration in Africa had to pack up and go, there followed a steady deterioration in social and economic stability, all of which was grist to the Communist mill.

It is useless to cry over spilt milk, so having accepted the fact of diminished power we have to calculate the minimum defensive strength which we and our allies can mobilize without the strain on our economies becoming intolerable.

The first resolution which we have to make is not to allow our eyes to be diverted from the main challenge of Russian communism; there are two areas in particular where the democracies could be vulnerable. The first is Europe and the Atlantic; the second the oil-producing area of the Gulf of Iran.

In the first case it is necessary to remember that the strength needed to deter a major power from aggression cannot be provided by Europe or America. Two wars have underlined that the minimum requirement is a combination of the power of both.

When therefore we ask what in present circumstances we should do, the plain answer is maintain the European–North American axis in NATO. That is a fundamental condition for survival.

Every now and again there are reports of alliance differences and of a faltering of will which do nothing to encourage confidence. Usually they have little substance, and I would

like to quote to you the recent verdict of Mr
Couve de Murville, a Prime Minister of France,
the ally which is popularly thought to be the
'wettest' when standing up to Communist
Russia.

He said: 'I have no hesitation in saying that
NATO's future is not in question. In short, the
Atlantic alliance remains in the present state of
the world the irreplaceable foundation of a
general equilibrium, failing which peace would
immediately be in danger'.

That is the sobering truth. Where else in the
world is there law and order, and comparative
political stability? I hope that your generation
will realize how lucky we are to live under the
umbrella of NATO, and will continue to equip
it with the minimum of force necessary to keep
the peace.

It will be necessary, until we can begin the
processes of disarmament, to add to our conventional weapons. That, though costly, is within our economic capacity. The Falkland Islands
campaign illustrated in miniature what military
skill, backed by the latest weapons which science
and technology have provided, can do, and
deterrence is better than a fight.

I shall resist the temptation to try and define
those weapons with which we should equip our-

selves. In that field the amateur is so easily con-
founded by the expert. But the general rule must
be to select those missiles which the enemy recog-
nizes as likely to penetrate the defences and break
up their plans for attack. That is not a static
position, so we must be ready to adapt to
changing needs.

The Middle East and the Gulf present a daunting problem. Oil is necessary in the modern
world for industry and for economic and social
stability, and if by political agitation the Communists could disrupt the supply to the developed
world, that would be for them a tempting and
glittering prize.

The United States has already given a public
warning to the Russians that the free flow of oil
from the Gulf of Iran is a vital interest to America,
while Germany and other countries of Western
Europe will be dependent on that area for the
greater percentage of their needs for a long time
to come.

Some have argued that NATO should enlarge
its horizons to include the defence of the sea
routes through the South Atlantic and round the
Cape of Good Hope into the Indian Ocean. It
would probably be unwise to involve the alliance
as such in that task, for it would be likely to

resurrect the charges of neo-colonization which would serve no useful purpose.

But should a challenge to the security of those sea passages be issued, the United States and Western Europe would have to see the tankers through. Indeed the British Government of 1970-74 took out an insurance policy against such an eventuality, when we made available the island of Diego Garcia as a base from which the allied navies could operate.

I was your age when I first began to understand the complexities of the politics of the Middle East. Mr Arthur Balfour was a friend of my father, and his famous declaration in 1917 in favour of a homeland for the Jews has been a subject of controversy all these years. Did he mean a place in which Jews could live at peace with their Arab neighbours? or did he foresee the formation of a State of Israel? I have never been able to make up my mind.

One of 'The Souls' – a group of particular cronies, described Balfour's ideas as being as 'imponderable as gossamer and dew' and perhaps he was not sure of his goal. He had, I remember, an acute and droll sense of humour. Surrounded by reporters, anxious to get his impression on descending from the Empire State Building in

New York, he is reported to have said: 'They tell me that this building is indestructible by fire, which I am bound to confess is a very great pity'! He was the first to convince me that politics could be fun.

However I am bound to admit that his formula for co-existence between Jews and Arabs was less than precise. He was, after all, the author of a work 'In defence of philosophic doubt'.

There was however one piece of cruel bad luck which distorted a conception that might otherwise have borne fruit, which was the wholesale ejection of the European Jews from Hitler's Germany. Their arrival in such numbers created the problem of the Palestinian refugees which is still with us today. These Jews had no doubt about their interpretation of the Balfour Declaration. Israel was to be a State in its own right, and so by the dedicated application of its people it became a member of the United Nations.

You have seen for yourself, in the evacuation of the Palestinians from Beirut, the military lengths to which Israel's leaders will go to secure that their identity is not threatened. Luckily for them the Arab countries have so far conspicuously failed to unite.

Religious wars with political overtones have always been characterized by excesses of cruelty, and this conflict between Arab and Jew is no exception.

It is too early to measure the effect of the scattering of the armed Palestinians among the other Arab countries, but I am afraid that in your life-time there will still be a large question-mark over the future of this area.

There are rumours of a Pan-Islamic movement which will be exclusive in its approach to international affairs. Who knows?

At any rate the absolute need of the West for another generation or so will be uninterrupted supplies of oil.

Arabs have an increasing affinity with Europe, and with quiet and sensitive diplomacy these life-lines, for they are no less, ought to remain secure.

Letter Eighteen

Nothing that I have written to you so far has given much ground for optimism. Count the wars in the world in my lifetime, or even in yours, and man's attitude to man is scarcely one of brotherly love.

Doubtless ordinary people everywhere long for peace, and it is the leaders who make the wars, but it is impossible to negotiate peace over their heads, and anyway to blame the top men seems to me to be too easy a way for the people to shuffle out of responsibility.

In the democracies we get the leaders we vote for, and therefore deserve, while totalitarianism is usually the penalty of neglect by ordinary men and women of their civic duties.

Can you in your lifetime expect any improvement in that dismal legacy?

My answer, I am bound to say, must be tentative. Undeniably man is made up from a mixture of good and evil. Even Christ did not promise perfection on earth, only redemption in a world

to come. Nevertheless Christians are commanded to try to live at peace with their neighbours, and to hope; so let us see if man has learned
any lessons from the past which can justify us in
looking forward to a brighter side to life?

Can we, for example, foresee any bridging of
the rift between the ideologies of Communism
and the practise of Capitalism, which has been
responsible for so many of the troubles of the
world?

You may perhaps have heard of Toynbee's
thesis in which he argues that when two philo-
sophies of life find themselves in conflict over a
period, each absorbs something of the other's
way of life. Certainly for better or for worse the
Western democracies have borrowed from
Marx's teaching, for the 'State' has been given
a significant rôle in their mixed economies.

Much more slowly, but yet noticeably, the
Communists are admitting that international
capital has a part to play in their industrial
development and growth. The Chinese have
openly admitted their need for it.

Hungary has diluted the Communist economic
doctrine, and demonstrably to her advantage,
while Roumania and Poland are clearly dis-
contented with their economic lot.

In Russia the economic revolution has had a

fair trial over more than fifty years, and it is now undeniable that there has been spectacular failures. Large quantities of grain have to be imported from North America and the Argentine to feed the Russian population; a project like the Siberian-European gas pipe-line cannot be undertaken without Western technology; while the standard of living of the Russian worker is far inferior to that of his opposite number in Europe or America.

There must be a strong compulsion to switch a massive slice of the investment cake from the military to the civil, and it is possible that where moral considerations have fallen on deaf ears, economic shortages and want may force a change.

I hesitate to moralize further for there are too many motes and beams about in international affairs for that sort of self-confidence, but the young Russian is increasingly bound to see through the barbed wire and the propaganda, and recognize the truth of the contrast between the free and the restricted ways of life. Socialism has signally failed to deliver him the goods.

It will, I suggest, pay the democracies to play the game of co-existence long.

The state of the economy is normally the prime concern of the government of any country, but Communist Russia's policies have contained such a high political content that the question must be whether the Politburo will allow economic considerations to dilute the fervour of pure doctrinal Communism.

Recently the Russian leaders should have learned a few lessons. The invasion of Afghanistan was a costly blunder. Thereafter Russia could no longer pose as a champion of the Third World countries; while inside Russia the war is unpopular with the conscripted soldiers who have been brought from Latvia, Esthonia and Lithuania. Afghanistan was followed by the pressure publicly exerted on Poland, which it was clear to everyone only just stopped short of occupation. Lately, too, when faced with situations of revolution and conflict, of which she would previously have taken immediate advantage, it is noticeable that Russia's actions have faltered.

It is, as we have seen, too early to conclude that Communist Russia has ceased to be dangerous, but neither economically nor politically is everything going her way.

The Western allies have taken the precaution to warn her clearly that interference with the freedom of the European and Atlantic areas, and interruption of the oil routes, would be acts amounting to war, so that Russia's leaders know what to avoid.

If the Kaiser was left in doubt in 1914, or Hitler in 1939, that is not true of Mr Andropov or his colleagues.

Prophecy in politics is an unrewarding exercise, but it may be that in the various difficulties which Russia is experiencing her leaders will decide to mark time.

I would expect them to continue political agitation in the area of Iran, Pakistan and the Gulf, but even then it is possible that they will only succeed in burning their fingers. Southern Africa too will be a target, but that is a far distant continent, and Russians are ignorant of Africa's ways. In Europe, always providing that NATO remains solid, I would expect the Russians to look for compromise.

In my next letter I will explore the possibility that they might even do so in the field of disarmament. There are those who say that since the arms are there on both sides they are bound to be used. I do not agree. Aggression is not an automatic consequence of arms, it is an attitude of mind.

Letter Nineteen

If you will look back at one of my earlier letters you will find that in the context of conventional weapons I put the words 'arms control' before disarmament. I did so because the Russians, with their suspicions of the motives of all foreigners, may continue to play out the game of 'mutuality' and 'balance' until the Greek Kalends.

They will bring into the argument the complication of their long frontier with China to make the equation between NATO and the Warsaw Pact even more of a puzzle. Then they will raise the problems posed by categories of weapons.

For example, are Russia's missiles beyond the Ural mountains 'strategic' or are they to be counted as weapons to be used in support of their armies in Eastern Europe? Likewise, what label is to be attached to the American missiles based in Britain, and to the French and British nuclear deterrents?

Then there is the proposal for nuclear free

zones. History teaches us that a vacuum of power is an invitation to aggression, but if there is merit in the suggestion, then which areas of Europe and the Soviet should be so defined? Such ideas should certainly be studied, but I am wondering whether there is not some preliminary action which could be taken which would build confidence and therefore help the parties in negotiation to come to practical decisions in the field in a shorter time-scale. The secret of any successful disarmament has always been the 'verification' of the measures agreed. During the years when I was negotiating it was called 'inspection' and Russia's face was set adamantly against it.

Lately, however, I have noticed that in the context of nuclear installations the Russian leaders have begun to talk very tentatively about the possibility of 'on-site inspection'. The Russians set a lot of store by words as they concern their own behaviour, and this could herald a change of attitude. Having steeled themselves to use the forbidden word it is possible that they will face up to action. If so, that could revolutionize the control of armaments prospect.

It is of course already true that we photograph each other's military installations from satellites in space, and they reveal considerable detail, but how much more satisfactory it would be if an agreed and regular procedure of verification and interpretation of photography for East and West could be adopted.

NATO would not be asking the Russians to concede anything which the allies are not prepared to apply to themselves, for inspection has been conceded by the West long ago. Such a programme would begin to rebuild confidence faster than anything else, and could pave the way for the actual reduction of forces and weaponry on the ground.

Two more things could be done. The first an extension of the existing notification of troop movements in relation to military manoeuvres. You were able a short time ago to see how the Argentinians used them to cover up the preparations for a real attack. In future such arrangements for exchanges of information must be foolproof.

Secondly 'site inspection' would enable everyone to confirm that the nations which have signed the Test Ban Treaty, and the Nonproliferation Treaty, were honouring the pledges they have given.

It may sound odd to you, but I am less concerned with the nuclear than I am with the build-up of conventional forces and arms. It is becoming so plain that a nuclear war would bring wholesale destruction to the combatants, and to others far removed from the battle-field that everyone is shying away from the prospect.

The Russians will not use a first-strike. What could they gain? There is loose talk that they might attack, relying upon the Americans, French and British declining to retaliate because that would mean suicide. That sort of argument is too clever by half. Free people are not ready to acquiesce in the destruction of their way of life by an alien aggressor.

No. A war is more likely to start because the Russians calculate that it would be safe to use their strength in conventional arms to gain a tactical prize in Europe, or to blockade essential supplies by sea.

Arms control and disarmament therefore must cover all deployment of forces and weapons of war.

So let us start with arms control and so on.

Jowitt, the famous Master of Balliol, once gave the following advice to a young man. 'Don't expect too much, and don't attempt too little.' That almost exactly represents my approach to disarmament negotiations with the Soviet Union.

Letter Twenty

Have we, I wonder, accumulated enough hard evidence from the past to arrive at a rough estimate of the chances of you and your contemporaries riding out your lives in peace?

From my story it would seem that your best course will be to hope for the best, and prepare for the worst. But I feel that that is too gloomy, and I prefer Jowitt's recipe for living.

I would not expect the Russian Communists to abandon their political activity of subversion of other ways of life. The international scene is too full of pots which are simmering and ready to be stirred for her to resist that temptation.

I would expect trouble in the area of Iran, Pakistan and the Gulf, and increasing activity in Southern Africa, but Russia's touch is less sure than it was, and her potential dupes and victims are more alert.

Nor would I expect her to risk a major war. Russia possesses the whole range of nuclear weapons, and her leaders know their capacity for destruction, and that the Western armoury could render Russia virtually uninhabitable should war come. It is also true that things are not running Russia's way, and war would be no answer to her troubles. Their élite have too much to lose.

Nevertheless the democracies must not rely on the existing stale-mate, for that would be to 'attempt too little'. The NATO countries, having taken the decision to contrive a balance of power which is real, must take the initiative with proposals for arms control and disarmament. I feel that there may well be a response.

What are the reasons for my comparative optimism?

They consist of a number of observable trends.

The Russian Communist revolution is now more than sixty years old, and economically and politically as we have seen it has not come up to its people's expectations. The satellites of Eastern Europe are beginning to question its economic performance, and they are finding its authoritarian attitude irksome.

Poland is on the brink of revolt, and the whole of the Eastern European 'cordon-sanitaire' is becoming a liability rather than an asset. Russia's lines of communication to the West are now clearly vulnerable.

China, too, has to be watched, and even in her present state of military weakness, presents to Russia the classic dilemma of a potential army on both flanks.

Nor, following the take-over of Afghanistan, has Russia gained the ascendancy for which she was looking in the Third World.

I remember in the first world war Sir Douglas Haig used to say that generals ought to remember that their opposite numbers were having trouble on the other side of the hill. While keeping up our guard we should conduct relations with the Russians as normally as they will allow us to do. I would not officiously offer them access to information about the most advanced computers and the technology which would assist their armament programme, but I would trade with them in grain and pipelines and the ordinary contacts which nations conduct with one another.

The struggle to induce the Russians to co-operate in peaceful co-existence has been a marathon. I hope you will persevere and see it through. The recipe is to combine prudence (not expecting too much) with initiatives, (not attempting too little) and my forecast is that you and yours will survive.

Letter Twenty-one

I feel that the classic 'Marathon' is a fitting description of the contest with Communism which has already lasted a lifetime, and in which the prize for showing stamina is the preservation of a way of life.

That raises the struggle above the Tweedle-dum/Tweedledee battle to a level which involves a moral issue.

Did you see the film 'Chariots of Fire'? On the face of it the story was no more than that of a match between two champion athletes; the sort of thing which we often see in the various 'Games' held around the world, in which no sooner is one record made than it is eclipsed by another. But here there was a difference. One of the young men would not train nor race on a Sunday because to do so offended against his Christian principles, and for them he was ready to forfeit the prizes of Olympus. His rival was a Jew, deeply understanding of the wrestling with his conscience with which his friend was engaged, yet all out to win. I am not introducing this picture as a commercial for Christianity, still less for Scotsmen (for Liddell was one) but as a reminder that there are certain values which are more precious than any material reward, and may be than life. They include such things as justice; freedom of speech and choice; tolerance and human rights.

The form of Socialism, adopted by the Soviet Union in their blueprint for revolution could once have been represented as akin to pure Christianity. Everyone was to share equally in the production, distribution and consumption of wealth, and life in Russia was to be fair and just. It was the ideal of the Israelis' Kibbutz magnified to a gigantic scale.

Of course the Communists did without a God, so that their only terms of reference for values were derived from man.

So far man-made Utopia has failed, and Russia's experiment is no exception. Lenin may possibly be given the benefit of the doubt, but Stalin was a monster corrupted by greed.

In theory a benevolent dictator is a possibility, although he has yet to be found, but Stalin drained Communism of any ideals with which it may have started, and substituted the creed of power – naked and ruthless power.

The flaw in Socialist philosophy has been the belief in the infallibility of the State in terms of the public good. In Russia its doctrinal enforcement has meant that in the name of the State the freedoms of the individual which make life worth living have been crushed to a point where it is miraculous that the spirit of man has survived. No democracy could accept a creed which does its best to squeeze all traces of individuality out of its subjects.

But – and this question must be asked – is this a case of the pot calling the kettle black? Does Christianity and democracy and the conception of the maximum of freedom with the minimum of law entitle us to claim a moral and a material superiority? Certainly not if our intention was to enforce it on the Communist world. That however is not our aim. We accept the injunction of non-interference in another nation's affairs. To do otherwise would be to fall into the error of which we accuse the Communist.

What virtues can we claim? First, I would place the Code of Conduct laid down by the Christian religion which insists that in relation to one's neighbour there must be restraint in the use of power. We err in the application to our affairs of the Sermon on the Mount, but we broadly accept the theme as our guide.

Secondly, we consult the majority of an adult electorate before laws are made in their name, and we seek to protect the rights of minorities in their making. That is the essence of democracy.

Thirdly, Parliament insists on free speech.

These things do not represent a difference of degree from Communism, they are a difference of principle and of kind.

The economic performance of what is known as Capitalism needs closer examination. Doubtless its operations are far from perfect (unemployment is a constant reminder of that), but in terms of material advance as measured in the consumer societies the democracies are streets ahead of the Communist state.

There is too in the democracies a floor below which public conscience will not allow the individual in misfortune to fall.

The real test is whether any individual in the free world would willingly transfer his life to the Soviet Union, and the answer to that would be an almost universal 'no'.

So I believe that a Christian and a democratic society is the best design for living.

I once asked a young immigrant who had been in Australia for a year how he liked the country. He replied, 'It's grand, you see tomorrow is always better than today.'

I doubt if you will be able to make that boast.
People in your generation will have to face
dilemmas and take decisions just as daunting as
those experienced by the statesmen of my time.
But there is no justification for settling down
into a rut of pessimism from which we talk our-
selves into decline. It will need sustained forti-
tude, but at least let us try in this country to make
that young pioneer's optimism come true.

POSTSCRIPT

My introduction to these letters now seems to have been many moons away, but I recall that I asked the question whether it sounded like the production of one who was a period piece and a pessimist who had got out of bed on the wrong side? I added that I would plead guilty to those charges if, when we came to the postscript, I could detect no hope of better things to come for you and your generation.

Well, I don't quite know why, but today I am not quite so glum.

It is true that one cannot open a newspaper without reading of some new horror; it is true that the Russians are still as exasperating in negotiation; true, too, as the Lebanon has recently proved, that man can still be sadistic and brutal. True, also, that almost every day one prays to be saved from one's friends who march around with their heads in the upper air, and refuse to admit that nuclear weapons have to be the subject of hard bargaining with those whose values are totally different from our Christian yardsticks, if disarmament is to be secured and peace to be built on a sure foundation.

Nevertheless a stubborn optimism persists.

I think that my mood follows from another rhetorical question which I asked in the same letter. 'Has man learnt anything at all in 2,000 years?'

I now believe that I can answer 'yes' at least in part.

China has recognized that to be a neighbour of Communist Russia does not mean security; America has learned that it is better to throw her weight into the balance of power early rather than late; Europe is learning the virtue of political unity; while men and women East and West are beginning to insist that weapons which threaten the extermination of millions must not be used, and the world has to find some better answer than deterrence.

Heaven knows that that conclusion is a modest enough advance, but it is something if that is the verdict reached by those who own the weapons and know their potential.

I am not sure that the Russians have yet brought themselves to admit the validity of mutual and balanced disarmament over the whole field of weaponry, but if I could listen at the Kremlin keyhole I suspect that I would hear the argument swinging that way.

That is a slender thread on which to build hope, but you will see from my narrative that I have never before felt able to go so far.

Let me put it this way. I still take out an insurance policy, but with less expectation of a crash.

I remember that I told you at the start not to answer until you had read the last of my letters. More than sixty years separate us, and I look forward to your reactions to my account of the events of those times, and to your verdict on them.

Is it a dirty trick to ask what you would have done differently? – and where would you go from here?